MEAT &
TWO VEG

FOR MEAT LOVERS EVERYWHERE

MEAT & TWO VEG

FIONA BECKETT

Absolute Press

First published in Great Britain in 2006 by
Absolute Press
Scarborough House
29 James Street West
Bath BA1 2BT
Phone 44 (0) 1225 316013
Fax 44 (0) 1225 445836
E-mail info@absolutepress.co.uk
Website www.absolutepress.co.uk

Publisher Jon Croft
Commissioning Editor Meg Avent
Art Direction Matt Inwood
Publishing assistant Meg Devenish
Photography Jason Lowe
Home Economist Claire Ptak
Stylist Cynthia Inions

A catalogue record of this book is available from the British Library

ISBN: 1904573541
ISBN 13: 9781904573548

Printed and bound by Printer Trento, Italy

A note about the text
This book is set in Helevetica Neue. Helvetica was designed in 1957 by Max Miedinger of the Swiss-based Haas foundry. In the early 1980s, Linotype redrew the entire Helvetica family. The result was Helvetica Neue.

CONTENTS

INTRODUCTION

THE GREAT BRITISH TRADITION OF MEAT & TWO VEG

Look at the on-line guides for foreigners visiting the UK for the first time and they will often explain – slightly disparagingly – that the English national diet is based on 'meat and two veg'. Obviously they relied for that information on books that were published shortly after the Second World War but in many ways it's still true – meat and two veg do have a unique place in our affections. And for most Brits of a certain age there's a reassuring familiarity about the phase and a nostalgia for the meals they were brought up on that makes it a profoundly comforting notion.

But what does meat and two veg represent these days? What veg, for a start? Most people, when I asked them, said 'peas and carrots', other suggestions were beans, sprouts and cabbage. The vexed question is whether you can legitimately call a meal 'meat and two veg' if one of the vegetables is potato? Or, if you don't count potatoes, is it enough for the second vegetable to be in the meaty component of the dish like mushrooms in a mushroom sauce or onions and peppers in a casserole?

Purists would, I suspect, say no but I take a more relaxed view of the matter. It's the overall effect and the spirit of the dish that counts. In the post-war era, when meat and two veg reigned supreme, the vegetables were there for a reason – to pad out heavily rationed and scarce meat. Now there's no need to do that but they still add vital balance, turning what might otherwise be a protein- and carbohydrate-heavy meal into a perfectly healthy one – and in terms of that objective it doesn't matter whether they're in the main recipe or on the side.

What does matter is the overall spirit of the dish. You could legitimately say a chicken stir-fry or a spaghetti bolognese, if it contained enough vegetables and was accompanied by a salad, was meat and two veg but that wouldn't be right. Meat and two veg is a very British concept so I've stuck by and large to the great stalwarts of the British culinary repertoire – roasts and grills, casseroles and bakes – giving them, OK, a bit of a twist, or suggesting a less conventional vegetable accompaniment but essentially this is British food in all its glory.

And there's absolutely nothing wrong with that.

FIONA BECKETT, JULY 2006

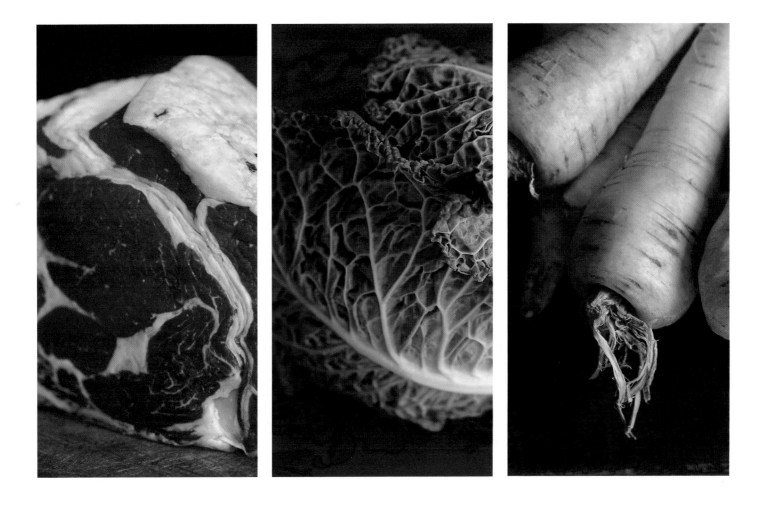

HOW TO BUY GOOD MEAT

When I first starting cooking in the 1970s, I used to be taken once a week by my mother-in-law to her local butcher. There we queued – invariably – until one of the rosy-cheeked, cheery and rotund (at least that's how I remember them) grey-haired men behind the counter would turn to us and say 'And what would you like today, Mrs B?'

'Corner wing rib' was my mother-in-law's favourite and I can remember the meat being ceremoniously presented, the flesh dark red and marbled with an edge of rich creamy fat. I was amazed she knew about this obscure cut that I had never heard of. Still more impressed when I got it home and cooked the best beef I had ever eaten.

Butchers like that still exist today (I go to two of them) but they're a dying breed. Yet we're the ones, I feel, who miss out, not only on that quality of meat but the banter and the chat. There's a real pride and craftsmanship there that is wonderful to see. I still love to watch my butcher, Barry, patiently and slowly score the rind of a piece of pork, the thinly-spaced, ruler-straight lines ensuring perfect crackling (and see p100 for Barry's cooking tips).

Butchers too are a reliable source of the less glamourous cuts of meat that have all the flavour. Beef skirt for pasties (or flashy French 'bavette' steak), chunky cubes of pork shoulder for long slow cooking, crumbly white suet-crusted lambs kidneys – it doesn't have to cost a fortune to eat well.

Thankfully for those who don't have a butcher of the old school or who don't have time to linger and admire their handiwork, anyone is now within reach of good meat simply by clicking a mouse. Even small producers like Brown Cow Organics and The Well Hung Meat Company now have highly professional websites that are easy to navigate and full of recipes and cooking tips (see p154). Many sell rare breed meat that doesn't even find its way onto the butcher's counter. Northfield Farm, for example, offers Dexter beef, Pedigree Meats offer Middle White pork and the Well Hung Meat Company superb Poll Dorset lamb. For the increasing numbers who are concerned about animal welfare they can tell you exactly how their meat is reared, what it has been fed on and how long it has been hung. Many of the same producers also turn up at farmer's markets. These markets have brought good old-fashioned locally produced food back within many more people's reach.

The quality and range of supermarket meat has also significantly improved. Sure, some of their meat is poor – tough, flavourless and of dubious provenance – but there are premium ranges like Jamie Oliver's range of 21-day aged beef for Sainsbury's or Waitrose's Poulet d'Or chicken, from meat produced on farms that are as good as you'll find in many local butchers.

It's not widely known but West Country branches of Sainsbury's have their own in-store meat counter run by Newton Abbot-based butcher Steve Turton. My local Budgens makes a feature of the sourcing of its British-produced meat. Even cut-price supermarket Morrison's has a good range of offal and other cheaper cuts like skirt. If you look out for good meat you'll find it.

WHICH CUT TO USE

Which meat you choose is going to depend primarily on your budget, how much time you've got and how health-conscious you are. If you're cooking a celebratory meal for family or friends, for example, you'll probably feel inclined to splash out on a rib of beef or leg of lamb. If you have time to cook you might settle for a slow-roast belly of pork or lamb shoulder. If you don't like fat on your meat – well, you probably shouldn't have bought this book for a start – but you may be looking for a lean pork or lamb steak you can cook quickly with the minimum of added fat. Some cuts can take being cooked quickly others need to be cooked slowly. Here's roughly what's suited to what.

ROASTING

If you want to cook a joint quickly go for a prime cut. Cheaper cuts generally need a longer cooking period.

BEEF
PRIME CUTS
Sirloin, fore rib, wing rib, fillet
CHEAPER CUTS (FOR POT ROASTING)
Topside, silverside, brisket

LAMB
PRIME CUTS
Saddle, leg, loin, rack of lamb
CHEAPER CUTS
Shoulder, breast

PORK
PRIME CUTS
Loin, leg
CHEAPER CUTS
Belly, hand, shoulder, spare rib

CHICKEN
PRIME CUTS
Whole organic birds
CHEAPER CUTS
Legs, thighs, drumsticks

FRYING & GRILLING

For frying and grilling you need lean cuts that will cook quickly.

BEEF
PRIME CUTS
Fillet steak, sirloin steak, rib eye steak
CHEAPER CUTS
Rump steak, skirt, 'minute' steak

LAMB
PRIME CUTS
Leg 'steaks', 'noisettes', cutlets, loin chops
CHEAPER CUTS
Chump chops, lamb fillet

PORK
PRIME CUTS
Pork fillet/medallions, escalopes, loin chops, steaks
CHEAPER CUTS
Loin chops and steaks can also be quite inexpensive, depending on the breed and whether or not they're organic

CHICKEN
PRIME CUTS
Breasts, fillets
CHEAPER CUTS
Legs, thighs

BRAISING, STEWING & CASSEROLES

The ideal use for tougher cuts of meat that have connective tissue that only breaks down with long slow cooking.

BEEF
Chuck steak, leg, shin, oxtail, mince

LAMB
Shoulder, lamb shanks, fillet, neck, mince

PORK
Spare rib chops, shoulder, chaps, mince

CHICKEN
Legs and thighs

HOW TO STORE FRESH MEAT

Some of the meat you buy will probably be vac-packed or tightly wrapped in clingfilm. If you're not going to eat it within a few hours unwrap it as soon as you get home, transfer it to a plate, cover it loosely with greaseproof paper or light aluminium foil and store it in the coldest part of the fridge. Perishable cuts such as mince and offal should be eaten the day you buy them. Others, such as larger joints, can be kept for a couple of days, depending obviously on how fresh they are when you buy them.

If you have stored joints or pieces of meat for longer than a few hours they will need patting dry with kitchen paper before you cook them (particularly important with steak or it won't brown).

SHOPPING FOR VEG

The vegetables that were served at the height of the meat-and-two-veg era weren't that varied but they were generally local and seasonal. Unlike today, when vegetables are flown halfway round the world so that we can have anything we want at any time of year.

Farmer's markets have undoubtedly created a higher awareness of what's in season, but longer growing seasons and new varieties have blurred the traditional harvesting periods. For example, these days the British asparagus season extends well into June, while Jersey potatoes, once a midsummer treat, can now be bought as early as April.

It's worth buying seasonally and locally not just because food is fresher and tastes better but because seasonal vegetables go naturally with the sort of food you want to eat at particular times of year. Spring vegetables like broad beans and peas are just perfect with the new season's lamb while root vegetables like carrots and parsnips are made for rich meaty stews.

Vegetables simply don't taste as good out of season. Watercress – freshly picked in summer is one of my favourite salad vegetables, but tastes of nothing in November. Leeks are dull as ditchwater in June. In fact they're dull full stop if you buy them washed and trimmed. All the flavour is in those rich green outer leaves.

Convenience is also the enemy of tasty vegetables. By the time they have been washed and sliced there's little character or nutritional value left – frozen peas excepted. Much better to buy them whole or with a little soil still clinging to them – they only take a few minutes to scrub or peel.

As with meat, I try to shop locally. Greengrocers are even thinner on the ground than butchers but many farm shops now sell their own vegetables. I currently buy regularly from a local nursery that grows a small selection – not organic but freshly picked that day – and once a month from my local farmer's market. I have tried veg boxes but I find their quality variable and the amount they include of each vegetable isn't always enough to do much with. I like to see and handle what I'm buying wherever possible.

A meal can be just as easily inspired by great vegetables as it is by a good joint of meat.

WHEN VEG ARE AT THEIR BEST

With most vegetables available year round it's a question of knowing when they're at their best rather than when they're in season. Obviously it will depend partly on the weather, the part of the country you live in, if you grow your own and the varieties you plant, but here's a rough guide:

POTATOES
NEW
April–August
MAINCROP
September–March

CARROTS
NEW SEASON
May–August
MAINCROP
September–March

PEAS
WHOLE PEAS FOR PODDING
May–July
SUGAR SNAP AND MANGETOUT
July–August

ONIONS
MAINCROP
August–March
SPRING ONIONS
May–September

BEANS
BROAD BEANS
May–June
FRENCH/WHOLE BEANS
July–September
RUNNER BEANS
July–August

BROCCOLI
PURPLE SPROUTING BROCCOLI
March–April

ORDINARY BROCCOLI
Year round but at its best from
June–September

CABBAGE AND GREENS
SPRING CABBAGE
May–June
SPRING GREENS
February–April
SAVOY CABBAGE
November–January
**RED CABBAGE
& OTHER VARIETIES**
November–March
KALE
October–April

TURNIPS
EARLY SEASON
June–July
MAINCROP
October–January

OTHER VEG
ASPARAGUS
May–June
AUBERGINES
August–September
BEETROOT

June–September
BUTTERNUT SQUASH
October–December
CAULIFLOWER
Like broccoli, available year round but
at its peak from July–September
CELERY
July–December, though it changes
from rich, leafy green celery in summer
to more delicate white celery in winter
CHICORY
October–November
COURGETTES
June–September
CUCUMBER
July–September
FENNEL
June–September
GARLIC
July–September
LEEKS
October–March
LETTUCE
June–August (obviously available at
other times of the year but lack texture)
MARROWS
July–September
MUSHROOMS
All year, though wild mushrooms

are best September–October
PARSNIPS
October–March
PEPPERS
August–October
SPINACH
June–September
SPROUTS
October–January
SWEDE
October–March
SWEETCORN
August–September
TOMATOES
July-September
WATERCRESS
May–July

HERBS
(The season for herbs can be extend-
ed by successive sowings)
BASIL
July–August
CHIVES, TARRAGON
May–June
MINT AND PARSLEY
May–September
ROSEMARY, SAGE AND THYME
Year round, best spring and summer

A NOTE ON STORING & COOKING

Few vegetables benefit from being stored for any length of time – like cheese, it's better to buy them a couple of times a week. If they have already been refrigerated or stored in an air-conditioned supermarket – the effect of which is much the same – they'll need to be kept in the fridge, otherwise their condition will deteriorate quite quickly. If they were sold in a plastic bag, break it open slightly so that moisture does not accumulate in the bag and rot the contents.

Root vegetables that are bought loose, particularly if they have dirt still clinging to them, will keep for a couple of days left in a rack in a cool place where air can circulate

round them. You should keep potatoes away from the light by storing them in a paper bag or sack. Tomatoes are better kept in a fruit bowl to continue ripening.

With one or two exceptions (potatoes being the most obvious example) vegetables are better cooked any way but boiled. Waterlogged cabbage and sprouts in particular are enough to put children off greens for a lifetime – and frequently do. Broccoli and cauliflower are better steamed; courgettes and squash better fried or baked. Even carrots are much more flavoursome cooked with just a spoonful or two of liquid (see p126). You simply don't need to drown them.

GRILLS & PAN-FRIES

SEARED FILLET STEAK WITH
ASPARAGUS AND MUSHROOMS

If you're making steak for more than two it's easier to finish it in the oven than cook them individually. This makes a great dinner party dish.

SERVES 4

1 tsp mixed peppercorns
$1/2$ tsp coarse sea salt
$1/2$ tsp dried rosemary
1 tsp plain flour
600g piece of fillet steak
1 tbsp olive oil
15g butter

FOR THE ASPARAGUS
AND MUSHROOMS

1 bunch of fresh asparagus
350g chestnut mushrooms
2 tbsp olive oil
25g butter
1 tsp balsamic vinegar
Salt and freshly ground black pepper

Preheat the oven to 230C/450F/Gas 8. Put the peppercorns, sea salt and rosemary in a mortar and crush to a fine consistency. Mix in the flour and tip into a shallow dish. Pat the steak dry and roll in the spice mixture. Heat a large frying pan for about 2 minutes, add the oil, heat for a minute then add the butter. As the foaming dies down place the steak in the pan and sear briefly on each side. Put the steak in a shallow dish or roasting tin and transfer to the oven for 10–15 minutes, depending how well done you like it. Remove and rest in a warm place for 10 minutes. Meanwhile trim the woody ends off the asparagus and cut them in two then cut the larger spears in half lengthways. Steam or microwave for 3 minutes until just tender. Wipe or rinse the mushrooms clean and slice roughly.

Heat a tablespoon of oil in the pan and toss the asparagus spears in it for a couple of minutes until they begin to brown and char. Remove from the pan and set aside. Add the remaining oil and butter and fry the mushrooms for 3–4 minutes. Return the asparagus to the pan and warm through. Season with a teaspoon of balsamic vinegar, salt and freshly ground black pepper. Pour any juices from the beef into the roasting pan then slice the beef thinly. Serve with a spoonful of juices poured over and with the asparagus and mushrooms alongside.

SAUTE POTATOES (p116) GO WELL WITH THIS – AND A DARK LEAFY GREEN SALAD IF YOU WANT EXTRA VEGETABLES.

STEAK DIANE

Now that waiters no longer flambé your steak at the table, Steak Diane has faded into a dim and distant memory. But resurrect it – it's a great steak dish for two.

SERVES 2

2 x thinly sliced sirloin steaks – about 175g each, trimmed of fat
1 tbsp light olive oil
40g soft butter
2 shallots or $\frac{1}{2}$ a small onion, peeled and very finely chopped
2 tsp Worcestershire sauce
2 tbsp dry Madeira
2 tbsp fresh beef stock
1 tbsp red or white wine vinegar
2 heaped tbsp roughly chopped flat-leaf parsley

Lay the steaks between two sheets of greaseproof paper and bash them out with a steak mallet or rolling pin. Season lightly with salt and pepper. Heat a large frying pan, add the olive oil then swirl it around and add half the butter. When the sizzling has died down lay the steaks in the pan and cook them for $1\frac{1}{2}$ minutes the first side then another 30 seconds to a minute the second side. Set aside on a warm plate. Tip the chopped shallot or onion into the pan and stir-fry for a minute. Add the Worcestershire sauce, Madeira, stock and vinegar and bubble up for a few seconds.

Turn the heat right down, add the remaining butter and whisk in. Pour any juices that have accumulated under the steaks into the pan and a splash of water if needed to thin the sauce. Season to taste with salt and pepper. Divide the steaks between two warm plates, pour the sauce over the top and scatter with the parsley.

CHIPS, **SAUTE POTATOES** (p116) OR **BAKED POTATOES** (p18) AND SOME GREEN BEANS GO WELL WITH THIS.

GRILLED LAMB STEAKS WITH LEMON, HONEY AND MINT

Many shops now sell nicely trimmed, lean lamb steaks that make a good quick mid-week supper.

SERVES 4

1 tsp clear honey
3 tbsp extra virgin olive oil
3 tbsp freshly squeezed lemon juice
1 clove of garlic, crushed
2 tbsp chopped fresh mint
4 lamb steaks, about 150g each

Spoon the honey into a shallow dish, add the oil and mix together with a wooden spoon. Add the lemon juice, garlic and mint and mix well. Trim any excess fat off the lamb steaks and place in the marinade, turning them so both sides are coated. Leave for about 30–45 minutes, turning the steaks a couple more times while they are marinating. When ready to cook them, heat a ridged grill pan for about 3 minutes until almost smoking. Remove the lamb steaks, shaking off any excess marinade and lay in the pan. Cook for 2–3 minutes depending on the thickness of the steaks then turn them over and cook for another 2–3 minutes depending how rare you like your lamb. Remove the lamb steaks and set aside on a plate to rest for 5 minutes. Remove the pan from the heat. Carve each steak at a slant into 3 thick slices and arrange on each plate. Pour any accumulated juices back into the pan along with the marinade and a splash of water, let it bubble up in the residual heat and pour the juices over the steaks.

PAN ROAST POTATOES (p116) AND A DARK, LEAFY GREEN SALAD GO WELL WITH THIS.

GRILLED LAMB CHOPS
WITH CRUSHED PEAS AND MINT

Sometimes you forget how good simple cooking and straightforward seasoning can be. I really don't think lamb chops need much more than salt and pepper, particularly when they've been cut from a homegrown new season's lamb. Don't be tempted to underdo them. Let the fat get nice and crispy – then you can eat it!

SERVES 2

4–6 evenly-sized lamb chops, about 2cm thick
1 tbsp olive oil
Salt and freshly ground black pepper

FOR THE CRUSHED PEAS
2 tbsp olive oil
Half a bunch of spring onions, trimmed and sliced
225g fresh or frozen peas
2 tbsp chicken or vegetable stock or 1 tsp vegetable bouillon powder and 2 tbsp water
2–3 sprigs of fresh mint
1 tbsp low-fat crème fraîche

Preheat the grill to high. Line the grill pan with foil and lay the chops on top. Trickle the oil over the top-side of the chops and season with salt and pepper. Grill just under the heat for about 5–6 minutes then turn the chops and season the other side. Cook for another 5–6 minutes then turn them again and give the first side another minute. While the chops are cooking, cook the peas. Heat a saucepan over a moderate heat and add the oil. Add the onions, stir and cook for a minute. Add the peas and stock. Put a lid on the pan, turn the heat down and cook for about 5–6 minutes or until the peas are tender. Wash the mint, strip the leaves off the stalks and shred finely. Stir into the peas, crushing them roughly with a potato masher or fork. Stir in the crème fraîche and season with salt and pepper.

THE OBVIOUS ACCOMPANIMENT WOULD BE SOME NEW POTATOES, TOSSED WITH BUTTER AND PARSLEY BUT YOU COULD SERVE SOME
BUTTERED SPINACH WITH NUTMEG (p134) AS WELL OR
INSTEAD. **GARLICKY GREEN BEANS** (p140) WOULD ALSO BE GOOD.

PICKLED PORK CHOPS
WITH SAGE AND ONION SPUDS

I owe the idea of brining pork chops to Guardian *cookery writer Matthew Fort, a man you can rely on to come up with the best possible way of cooking any given cut of meat. It makes even run-of-the-mill pork fabulously tender.*

SERVES 4

75g coarse sea salt
40g unrefined granulated or caster
   sugar
1/2 tsp black peppercorns
1/2 tsp juniper berries
A few allspice berries or a pinch of
   ground allspice
2 bay leaves
4 pork chops
2 tbsp light olive oil or sunflower oil
25g butter
Freshly ground black pepper

Measure out 1.5 litres of water into a saucepan. Add the salt and sugar and heat gently until both are dissolved. Add the peppercorns, juniper, allspice and bay leaves, stir and bring to the boil. Simmer for 5 minutes then remove from the heat and cool. Lay the chops in a single layer in a roasting tin or baking dish and pour over the brine and leave for 12 hours. Preheat the grill to high. Rinse the chops and pat them dry with kitchen paper. Heat the oil gently and add the butter. Put the chops in a grill pan, brush generously with the oil and butter mix, season with pepper and grill for 6–8 minutes, depending on the thickness of the chops. Turn the chops over and brush the other side with the oil and butter mixture, season and grill for another 6–8 minutes. Rest in a warm place for 5 minutes. Serve with the sage and onion spuds.

SAGE AND ONION SPUDS
600g washed new potatoes
3 tbsp light olive oil or sunflower oil
1 bunch of spring onions, trimmed
   and finely sliced
1 medium eating apple (e.g. Blenheim
   or Cox)
A small handful of sage leaves, woody
   stalks removed
Salt and pepper

Cook the potatoes in boiling water for 8–10 minutes or until just tender. Drain and cool slightly. Heat a large frying pan and add the oil and heat for about 2 minutes. Add the onions, apple and sage and stir-fry for a minute then slice the potatoes into the pan. Crush the potatoes with a wooden spoon or fork and fry for about 7–8 minutes, turning the mixture every couple of minutes. Season well with salt and pepper.

ANY KIND OF GREENS WOULD GO WITH THIS. **HOT BUTTERED CABBAGE** (p132), SPROUTS OR STEAMED BRUSSEL TOPS – IT'S UP TO YOU.

FRENCH-STYLE PORK WITH MUSHROOMS AND MUSTARD

This classic wine, crème fraîche and mustard-based sauce is quick, easy and versatile. You can equally well use it for chicken or turkey.

SERVES 2

1 tbsp olive oil
10g butter
2 boneless pork loin steaks (about 300g)
125g chestnut mushrooms, rinsed, trimmed and thickly sliced
1 level tsp flour
100ml white Burgundy or other dry white wine
1 tsp chopped fresh thyme leaves
2 tbsp crème fraîche
2 rounded tsp Dijon mustard
Freshly ground black pepper
Some scissor-snipped chives

Heat a medium-sized frying pan and add the oil. When it's hot add the butter then lay the pork steaks in the pan. Brown for about 3 minutes on each side, then turn the heat down and cook for a further 2–3 minutes on each side depending on the thickness of the steaks. Remove from the pan and keep warm. Cook the mushrooms in the remaining oil and butter until lightly browned. Scoop them out with a slotted spoon and add to the pork. Stir the flour into the pan then add the white wine and thyme and bubble up until reduced by about two thirds. Turn the heat right down and stir in the crème fraîche then add the mustard and warm through taking care not to boil the sauce (which will make the mustard taste bitter). Season with black pepper then return the pork and the mushrooms to the pan. Heat through very gently then serve. Sprinkle with chives.

THIS GOES WELL WITH NEW POTATOES AND **A SIMPLE LETTUCE SALAD** (p150) OR **BUTTERED SPINACH WITH NUTMEG** (p134).

ITALIAN-STYLE PORK WITH TOMATO, CELERY AND LEMON

This Italian-inspired approach to pork makes a nice light summer supper.

SERVES 2

3 sticks of celery, trimmed and sliced
2 pork 'steaks', about 175g each
2 tbsp olive oil
1 medium onion, peeled and finely chopped
1 small clove of garlic, peeled and crushed
1 tsp tomato purée
75ml dry white wine
250g fresh tomatoes, skinned and roughly chopped
2 heaped tbsp chopped flat-leaf parsley
A little grated rind from an unwaxed lemon (about $1/4$ tsp)
Salt, pepper and sugar to taste

Put the celery in a small saucepan, pour in just enough boiling water to cover, add a pinch of salt and cook for 5 minutes. Drain the celery, reserving the cooking liquid. Pat the pork steaks dry with kitchen paper and season both sides with salt and pepper. Heat a medium-sized frying pan, add a tbsp of oil and lay the pork steaks in the pan. Brown for a minute or two then turn over and brown the other side. Turn the heat down and continue to cook until the pork is tender (another 3–4 minutes a side depending on the thickness of the steak and how dense the meat is). Remove from the pan and set aside. Add the remaining oil to the pan and fry the onion for 3–4 minutes until

beginning to soften. Stir in the garlic and tomato purée, cook for a minute then add the white wine and bubble up until it has reduced by half. Add the chopped fresh tomatoes, celery and 3–4 tbsp of the celery cooking liquid and continue to cook until the tomatoes have broken down and the sauce has become jammy in consistency. Season to taste with salt, pepper and a small pinch of sugar if you think it needs it, then stir in the parsley and lemon rind. Return the meat and any juices that have accumulated on the plate to the pan and warm through. Check the seasoning then serve the chops with the sauce spooned over.

A FEW **COURGETTE 'CHIPS'** (p146) ARE NICE WITH THIS, OR YOU COULD SERVE IT WITH NEW POTATOES. ALTERNATIVELY, ADD HALF A TIN OF WELL-RINSED HARICOT BEANS TO THE SAUCE TO MAKE IT MORE SUBSTANTIAL AND SERVE A SALAD WITH IT.

SMOKY BACON CHOPS
WITH GRILLED TOMATOES AND FRESH CREAMED CORN

Creamed corn sounds, well, corny but made with fresh corn it's actually quite delicious especially with a nice fat bacon chop. A good brunch dish for two.

SERVES 2

2 boneless smoked bacon chops or
   thick gammon steaks
2 tbsp sunflower or light olive oil
4 small to medium vine-ripened
   tomatoes, halved

FOR THE CREAMED CORN
2 corn on the cob
25g butter
2 tbsp whipping cream
Sea salt and cayenne pepper
1 tbsp roughly chopped flat-leaf
   parsley

First make the creamed corn. Remove the outer husk if it's still on the cob. Holding the cob base downwards on a chopping board, cut downwards with a small sharp knife to remove the kernels. Don't cut too deep. Take a metal teaspoon and scrape off the rest of the kernels and any juices into a bowl. Melt the butter in a small saucepan, add the cream and heat the kernels through gently for about 6–8 minutes until they have lost their raw taste but are still slightly crunchy.

Meanwhile heat a non-stick frying pan for 2–3 minutes until hot. Snip the fat on the bacon chops in a couple of places to stop them curling. Brush the chops and the cut halves of the tomatoes with the oil and lay them face downwards on the pan. Cook for about three minutes then turn over and cook the other side, pressing the chops down firmly with a wooden spatula so they stay flat. Season the creamed sweetcorn generously with salt and a little cayenne pepper and stir in the parsley. Serve alongside the bacon chops and tomatoes.

THIS RECIPE COMES WITH ITS OWN VEGETABLES BUT YOU COULD SERVE SOME NEW POTATOES WITH IT OR ADD SOME PEAS.

SAUTEED CHICKEN
WITH COURGETTES AND MINT

A simple summery weekday supper. Couldn't be easier.

SERVES 2

350g chicken fillets or 2 skinless, boneless chicken breasts
2 tbsp plain flour
3 tbsp olive oil
20g butter
2 large or 3 medium-sized courgettes (about 350g), trimmed and cut into small dice
$1/2$ a bunch of spring onions
2 heaped tbsp chopped fresh mint
1 lemon, cut into wedges
Salt and freshly ground black pepper

If you're using chicken breasts cut them in half lengthwise. Season the flour with salt and pepper and dip the fillets into the flour ensuring they are evenly coated. Heat a large frying pan and add 1 tbsp of the oil, then the butter. Fry the chicken fillets for about 2–3 minutes each side until lightly browned, turning them a couple of times. Set aside on a warm plate and cover lightly with foil. Pour the fat off the pan, wipe dry with kitchen paper and add the remaining oil. Tip in the diced courgettes and fry for a couple of minutes turning them regularly. Add the sliced spring onions and continue to fry until the courgettes are nicely browned and tender (about another 3–4 minutes). Stir in the mint, season with salt, pepper and a squeeze of lemon. Push the courgettes to the side of the pan and reheat the chicken fillets briefly. Serve the chicken fillets with the courgettes on the side and a lemon wedge to squeeze over.

I QUITE LIKE THIS AS A POTATO-LESS DISH WITH SOME STEAMED BROCCOLI ON THE SIDE BUT YOU COULD, OF COURSE, SERVE SOME NEW POTATOES.

DUCK WITH ORANGE AND REDCURRANT SAUCE

A simple but flashy-looking recipe harking back to the days when duck breasts always seemed to be served with some kind of fruit sauce. Tasting this you will see why.

SERVES 2

1 tbsp oil
A small slice of butter (about 15g)
2 skinless Gressingham duck breasts, about 150g each
3 tbsp Vintage Character or Late Bottled Vintage port
1 tbsp red or white wine vinegar
Juice of half an orange (about 2 tbsp)
$1/4$ tsp orange rind
2 tbsp redcurrant jelly
50g fresh or frozen redcurrants, de-stalked, or cranberries or halved and stoned cherries
Salt and freshly ground black pepper

Heat a small frying pan, big enough to take both duck breasts in a single layer, add 1 tablespoon of the oil, then the butter. Fry the duck breasts over a moderate heat for about 4–6 minutes each side (depending on size) until nicely browned, turning them a couple of times. Set aside on a warm plate and cover lightly with foil. Pour the remaining fat out of the pan and pour in the port and vinegar. Let it bubble up for a minute then add the orange juice and rind and redcurrant jelly. Reheat slowly until the redcurrant jelly melts then turn the heat up, add the redcurrants and simmer for a few seconds. Pour in any juices that have accumulated under the duck and check the seasoning, adding salt and pepper to taste. Slice the duck breasts diagonally, arrange on each plate and spoon over the sauce.

THIS TASTES GOOD WITH A FEW NEW POTATOES AND A DARK, GREEN LEAFY ROCKET OR WATERCRESS SALAD.

TURKEY ESCALOPES WITH LEMON, CAPERS AND ANCHOVIES

This harks back to a splendidly retro dish called Escalope of Veal Holstein – breadcrumbed veal fillets served with a topping of a fried egg, capers and anchovies. This is a lighter version that tastes pretty good with turkey fillets.

SERVES 2

250g thinly sliced turkey, chicken or veal escalopes
25g plain flour, seasoned with salt and pepper
1 egg, lightly beaten
40g natural dried breadcrumbs
4–6 tbsp light olive oil or sunflower oil
25g–40g butter
1 tbsp capers, rinsed, drained and chopped
2 anchovies, finely chopped
2 tbsp finely chopped parsley
1 tbsp lemon juice
1 hard boiled egg finely chopped (optional)

Place the turkey fillets between two sheets of greaseproof paper and beat out flat with a rolling pin. Put the flour, egg and dried breadcrumbs in 3 separate shallow bowls. Dip each turkey fillet in the seasoned flour, then in the beaten egg, shaking off any excess, finally in the dried breadcrumbs, making sure it has been evenly coated. Heat a frying pan, add 2 tbsp of the oil then add half the butter. Once the butter has melted lay the fillets in the pan and fry briefly for about $1\frac{1}{2}$ minutes each side until

nicely browned. Set aside on a warm plate. Do this in two batches if necessary, adding more oil and butter as you need it. Rinse and wipe the pan and replace over the heat. Pour in 2 tbsp of olive oil, warm through briefly then add the capers, anchovies, parsley and lemon juice. Bubble up for a minute. Divide the escalopes between two plates and spoon over the parsley and caper mixture. Sprinkle over a little finely chopped hard-boiled egg, if using.

SERVE WITH NEW POTATOES AND **BUTTERED SPINACH WITH NUTMEG** (p134) OR A SPINACH, ROCKET AND WATERCRESS SALAD.

SAUSAGE AND MASH WITH ONION, SAGE AND CIDER GRAVY

You can adapt your gravy to the style of sausage you're using. This suits simple old-fashioned British sausages or lighter sausages such as pork and leek. There are two other great gravy recipes on page 34.

SERVES 3–4

600g plain pork or pork and leek
  sausages
2 tbsp light olive oil or sunflower oil
800g King Edwards or other good
  boiling potatoes
25g soft butter
50ml warm milk
Salt and pepper

FOR THE GRAVY
2 tbsp light olive or sunflower oil
20g butter
2 large, mild Spanish onions (about
  425–450g), peeled and finely sliced
1 tsp finely chopped fresh sage
1 level tbsp plain flour
200ml fresh chicken stock
200ml dry cider
Salt and ground white pepper

Start the gravy by heating a large lidded saucepan or casserole over a moderate heat. Add the oil, heat for a minute then add the butter. When the butter has melted tip in the onions, stir thoroughly then put the lid on the pan and cook on a low heat, stirring occasionally, for about 15–20 minutes until the onions are soft and golden. Meanwhile peel the potatoes, cut into even-sized pieces, put in a pan, cover with cold water and bring to the boil. Cook for about 15–20 minutes until just tender. When the onions are ready, stir in the sage and cook for a few seconds then stir in the flour. Add the cider and stock, bring to the boil then turn the heat right down and simmer for 10 minutes. Heat the remaining oil and brown the sausages well on all sides. Remove from the pan, add to the gravy and continue to cook over a low heat for about 10 minutes. Drain the potatoes and mash thoroughly. Work in the warm milk and remaining butter and season with salt and pepper. Set aside and keep warm. Check the seasoning of the gravy, adding salt and white pepper to taste. Serve the sausages with the gravy spooned over accompanied by the mash.

PEAS WOULD BE TRADITIONAL. **HOT BUTTERED CABBAGE** (p132) IS GOOD TOO.

TWO OTHER GOOD GRAVIES TO GO WITH SAUSAGES

REAL ALE, BAY AND THYME GRAVY

Good with plain pork or herb sausages such as Cumberland or Lincolnshire.

1 tbsp oil
15g butter
2 medium onions, peeled and sliced
1 level tsp malt extract or soft brown sugar
1 tsp fresh thyme or 1/2 tsp dried thyme
1 level tbsp flour

175ml bottle-conditioned ale
200ml fresh beef stock or stock made with 200ml boiling water and 1 tsp Marmite
1 bay leaf
Salt, pepper and tomato ketchup to taste

Heat a saucepan or casserole over a moderate heat. Add the oil, heat for a minute then add the butter. When the butter has melted tip in the onions, stir thoroughly then cook over a moderate heat for 10 minutes until the onions start to brown. Stir in the malt extract or soft brown sugar and thyme, cook for a few seconds then stir in the flour. Cook for a minute then add the ale, stock and bay leaf, bring to the boil then turn the heat right down and simmer for 15–20 minutes, adding a little water if it gets too thick. Check the seasoning of the gravy, adding salt and pepper to taste and a little tomato ketchup (about a teaspoon) if you think it needs sweetening.

RED WINE AND ROSEMARY GRAVY

Particularly good with beef and venison sausages. You could also serve it with other beef or lamb dishes – it's good with a steak.

2 tbsp light olive oil or sunflower oil
20g butter
2 medium red onions, peeled and finely sliced
1 clove of garlic, peeled and crushed
1 tbsp finely chopped rosemary leaves

1 tbsp tomato purée
1 level tbsp plain flour
150ml full bodied red wine
250ml beef stock or stock made with 200ml of boiling water and 1 tsp Marmite
Salt, freshly ground black pepper and tomato ketchup to taste

Heat a saucepan or casserole over a moderate heat. Add the oil, heat for a minute then add the butter. When the butter has melted tip in the onions, stir thoroughly then cook over a moderate heat for 10 minutes until the onions start to brown. Stir in the garlic and rosemary, cook for a few seconds then stir in the tomato purée and flour. Add the red wine and stock, bring to the boil then turn the heat right down and simmer for 15–20 minutes, adding a little water if it gets too thick. Check the seasoning of the gravy and adding salt and pepper to taste and a little tomato ketchup if you think it needs sweetening. If you're serving this with a steak or roast you may want to strain it through a sieve.

STICKY 'BARBECUED' SAUSAGES

If you suddenly have a craving for a barbie and it's chucking it down outside, this is the recipe for you.

SERVES 2–3

1–2 tbsp sunflower oil or olive oil
450g premium pork sausages (plain, rather than flavoured)
1 small onion, peeled and finely chopped
1 clove of garlic, peeled and crushed
4 tbsp tomato ketchup
2 tbsp red or white wine vinegar
25g soft brown sugar
1 tsp English or Dijon mustard
1 tbsp Worcestershire sauce
A few drops of hot chilli sauce (optional)

Heat a medium-sized frying pan and add 1 tbsp of oil. Put the sausages in the pan and brown them on all sides (about 5–7 minutes). Remove them from the pan, add the extra oil if needed and add the chopped onion. Stir and cook for about 4–5 minutes until beginning to soften. Add the garlic, stir and cook for a minute then add the tomato ketchup, sugar, mustard, Worcestershire sauce and 2 tablespoons of water, stir well and bring to the boil. Return the sausages to the pan, turn them in the sauce then turn the heat right down and simmer for about 10 minutes until the liquid has almost evaporated from the pan and the sauce is beginning to stick to the side of the sausages. Check the seasoning, adding a few drops of chilli sauce if you want it hotter. (You shouldn't need salt or pepper.) Turn the heat off and leave the sausages for 5 minutes, turning them in the sticky goo, then serve.

SWEET POTATO WEDGES (p119) OR BAKED SWEET POTATOES WOULD BE GOOD WITH THIS DISH, TOGETHER WITH PEAS, BROCCOLI OR **GARLICKY GREEN BEANS** (p140).

LIVER AND BACON WITH PIQUANT TOMATO SAUCE

Piquant is a word that has all but vanished from our culinary vocabulary but it exactly describes the sharp, tangy taste of this gravy.

SERVES 2

2 tbsp plain flour
250g thinly sliced lamb's liver
3 tbsp light olive oil or sunflower oil
4 rashers of dry-cured back bacon
$\frac{1}{2}$ a glass (about 75ml) red wine
1 level tsp tomato purée
175ml ready-made beef stock or
   stock made with a third of an
   organic beef stock cube
A few drops of Worcestershire sauce
Salt and freshly ground black pepper

Season the flour with salt and pepper. Dip in the liver slices, thoroughly coating both sides. Heat a frying pan, add 2 tablespoons of the oil and fry the bacon rashers on both sides until starting to crisp. Set aside on a warm plate. Fry the liver in the oil for about a minute each side then set aside with the bacon. Tip the red wine into the pan and bubble up for a minute until reduced by half. Stir in the tomato purée then add the beef stock and bring to the boil adding a little water if the sauce is too thick. Add a few drops of Worcestershire sauce and simmer for a couple of minutes. There should be enough salt but you might want to add a little more pepper. Divide the liver and bacon between two plates, spooning the sauce over the liver.

SERVE WITH MASHED POTATO AND LIGHTLY STEAMED BROCCOLI.

SEARED CALF'S LIVER WITH GARLIC AND ANCHOVY BEANS

Calf's liver it has to be said, doesn't really suit traditional British liver cooking methods so here's an Italian-inspired way of cooking it that preserves its delicacy. You obviously don't have to use yellow beans but they are available in many farmers' markets nowadays and make the dish look great.

SERVES 2–3

FOR THE GARLIC AND ANCHOVY BEANS

175g each whole green beans and yellow beans or 350g green beans
2 tbsp extra virgin olive oil
3–4 anchovies
1 large clove of garlic, crushed
2 heaped tbsp chopped flat-leaf parsley

250–300g thinly sliced calf's liver
1 tbsp olive oil
20g butter
Salt and pepper

Top and tail the beans and blanch in boiling water until just tender (about 4 minutes). Drain and rinse with cold water. Snip the anchovies into small pieces. Heat the oil gently and cook the anchovies for a couple of minutes squashing them with a wooden spoon so they form a paste. Add the garlic and cook for a minute or two. Return the beans to the pan together with the chopped parsley and heat through for a couple of minutes. Set aside while you cook the liver.

To cook the liver, preheat a ridged grill until almost smoking (about 3 minutes). Melt the oil and butter in a small saucepan, brush over the surface of the liver and season with salt and freshly ground black pepper. Lay the liver pieces on the grill, cook for a minute until you see blood rise to the surface then turn over and cook another 30 seconds to a minute depending how well done you like it. Set aside on a warm plate and rest for 2–3 minutes before serving.

YOU COULD POP SOME CHERRY TOMATOES ON THE GRILL ONCE YOU'VE COOKED THE LIVER AND ROLL THEM AROUND TILL THEY'RE NICELY CHARRED.

SAUTEED LAMBS' KIDNEYS WITH GIN AND JUNIPER

Kidneys are an underrated delicacy. Try the ones that are still wrapped in their suet. Traditional butchers still stock them, though you may have to order them in advance.

SERVES 2

4–6 lambs kidneys, depending on size
2 tbsp flour, seasoned with salt and pepper
1 tbsp light olive oil or sunflower oil
20g butter
1 small onion, peeled and finely chopped
A small clove of garlic, crushed (optional)
125g chestnut mushrooms, rinsed and finely sliced
3 tbsp gin
1 level tsp juniper berries
A pinch of allspice (optional)
1 level tsp tomato purée
$\frac{1}{2}$ tsp sweet paprika
150ml chicken or vegetable stock made with 1 level tsp vegetable bouillon powder
5 tbsp double cream or crème fraîche
2 tbsp finely chopped fresh parsley
Salt and freshly ground black pepper

Remove any outer fat from the kidneys, cut them in half lengthways, peel away any skin and cut away the white core in the middle of each half. Thoroughly coat each piece in seasoned flour. Heat a frying pan, add the oil then add the butter. When the foaming dies down lay the kidney halves in the pan. Cook for about 2 minutes until the blood rises to the surface then turn them over and cook another minute. Remove from the pan with a slotted spoon. Add the onion, stir and cook for a minute or two then add the sliced mushroom and fry for 2–3 minutes. Add 2 tbsp of the gin and bubble up until evaporated, then add the crushed juniper, allspice if using, tomato purée and paprika. Stir and cook for a few seconds then add the stock and bring up to simmering point. Turn the heat down and return the kidneys to the pan and heat through without boiling for 2–3 minutes. Stir in the cream and season to taste with salt and freshly ground black pepper. Add the final spoonful of gin and a little extra water if the sauce seems too thick. Sprinkle with parsley and serve with rice.

A GREEN SALAD OR **ONE-MINUTE COURGETTES** (p147) MAKE A GOOD ACCOMPANIMENT.

STEWS, CASSEROLES & BOILED MEATS

STEAK, KIDNEY AND GAME PUDDING WITH EXTRA GRAVY

Steak and kidney pudding is an easy dish to make – it just takes ages to cook; a good 4–5 hours. You can vary the meat content (apart from the kidney which is vital for the gravy). I like to add some mixed game, duck or venison for a richer pud.

SERVES 6

400g ox kidney
400g good quality lean braising steak, cut into cubes
200–250g game pie mix or a duck breast or some venison, cut into cubes
3 level tbsp plain flour
1/4 tsp dried thyme
2 small onions, peeled and very finely chopped
300ml beef stock
300ml red wine plus a little extra to finish the gravy
2 tbsp sunflower oil or light olive oil
1/4 tsp Worcestershire sauce
1 tbsp tomato ketchup (optional)
Salt and freshly ground black pepper

FOR THE SUET PASTRY
350g self-raising flour
175g shredded beef suet
About 200ml cold water
Salt and freshly ground black pepper

You will need a large (1.5 litre) pudding bowl well greased with soft butter.

Cut up the kidney, cutting away the central white core and cut into small cubes. Set half aside for the gravy. Put the remaining half in a bowl with the cubed beef and game, sift over 2 tablespoons of flour, add the thyme, season well with salt and pepper and mix together. Add half the chopped onion and mix again. To make the pastry, put the rest of the flour in a large bowl and season with salt and pepper. Add the suet and cut it into the flour with a round-bladed knife. Stir in the water gradually, bringing the pastry together with a knife and then your hands until it forms a ball that leaves the side of the bowl clean. Roll it out lightly on a floured work surface or board into a circle large enough to line the basin. Cut away just over a quarter of the pastry in a large slice for the lid then carefully fit the rest into the buttered basin, damping the cut edges to seal them together and making sure the base is leak-proof. Spoon the filling into the pastry. Mix together the beef stock and red wine and pour in enough to come just below the top of the meat, set the rest aside for extra gravy. Roll out the remaining pastry so it will cover the pie and lower on top of the filling.

Dampen and press the edges together and trim off any pastry that overhangs the rim. Cover the pudding with a pleated layer of baking parchment and tie securely with string, then a pleated layer of extra thick foil, again, tied tightly with string, leaving a 'handle' across the top of the pudding so you can lift it easily. Put an upturned plate or saucer in the bottom of a large saucepan, perch the pudding on top and carefully fill the pan with boiling water about half way up the side of the pudding bowl. Put a tight-fitting lid on the pan and steam for about 4 1/2 hours, topping up the water occasionally.

Meanwhile make the extra gravy. Heat a saucepan and add 2 tbsp of oil, cook the onion for about 3–4 minutes until soft. Add the remaining chopped kidney and fry for a couple of minutes until lightly browned. Sprinkle with the remaining flour, season and cook for a minute, then add the remaining stock and wine mix and bring to the boil. Simmer for about an hour then set aside until ready to use. Strain the gravy, return it to the pan and add the Worcestershire sauce, an extra splash of wine and a little tomato ketchup if needed to round out and sweeten the flavour. Serve the pudding from the bowl, pouring extra gravy over each portion.

BRAISED CARROTS (p126) AND **STEAMED CABBAGE WEDGES** (p133) ARE PERFECT WITH THIS.

BEEF STEW WITH CHIVE AND PARSLEY DUMPLINGS

The stew is based on an old Arabella Boxer recipe from a handy little book called Christmas Food and Drink *published in 1975.*

SERVES 4

900g braising beef (800g if you buy it ready-trimmed)
25g plain flour
40–50g beef dripping or light olive oil
2 large onions (about 350–400g in total), peeled and sliced
350g carrots, peeled and sliced
300ml dry or medium dry cider
300ml beef or chicken stock
2 tbsp cider vinegar
1 bay leaf
Salt and freshly ground black pepper

FOR THE CHIVE AND PARSLEY DUMPLINGS
200g self-raising flour
1 tsp baking powder
$\frac{1}{2}$ level tsp mustard powder
$\frac{1}{2}$ level tsp fine sea salt
$\frac{1}{8}$ tsp white pepper
75g suet
1 heaped tbsp finely snipped chives
1 heaped tbsp finely chopped parsley
125–150ml iced water

If the meat is not already prepared trim off any excess fat and cut into large cubes. Put the flour in a bowl and season with salt and pepper. Dip the meat in the flour, shaking off any excess. Heat a large frying pan and add half the beef dripping or oil. Fry the meat, browning it well on all sides, adding extra dripping if needed. (You should be able to do this in two batches.) Transfer the meat to a lidded casserole with a slotted spoon. Add the remaining dripping to the frying pan and fry the onions gently for about 7–8 minutes, turning them regularly, then add the carrots, stir and cook for another 5 minutes. Tip the vegetables on top of the meat. De-glaze the pan with the cider, add the beef or chicken stock and cider vinegar and bring to the boil. Pour the liquid over the stew, stir well and bring the whole stew to the boil. Skim off any froth, add the bay leaf, cover and cook over a very low heat for about $2\frac{1}{2}$ hours.

To make the dumplings, sieve the flour, baking powder, mustard and salt into a bowl. Tip in the suet and cut it in with a sharp knife. Mix in the herbs then gradually add enough cold water to hold the mixture together, without working the mixture too much. Form the dough into 8–10 small balls and lay on the top of the casserole. Replace the lid and continue to simmer for 15 minutes. Remove the lid and cook for another 5 minutes to allow the dumplings to dry a little.

SERVE WITH STEAMED GREENS OR BRUSSEL TOPS.

BRAISED BEEF WITH PORT AND PORTER AND MASHED SWEDES

This deliciously, comforting old-fashioned dish is adapted from an old recipe called Sussex Stew that was included by Elizabeth David in her Spices, Salts and Aromatics in the English Kitchen. A good recipe to make just after the Christmas holiday when you're sick to death with turkey and have some leftover port to use up.

SERVES 4–6

1.25kg leg of beef (shin) in one piece
2 tbsp plain flour
1/2 tsp ground allspice
1 large onion, peeled and roughly chopped
2 bay leaves
100ml Vintage Character or Late Bottled Vintage port plus a little extra to finish the dish
175ml porter or stout
125ml beef stock or stock made with 1/2 tsp Bovril
2–3 tbsp mushroom ketchup or malt vinegar
Salt and freshly ground black pepper

FOR THE MASHED SWEDES

1 medium to large swede (about 1kg), peeled and cut into large chunks
1 litre light vegetable stock
About 25g butter
Salt and freshly ground black pepper

Preheat the oven to 140C/275F/Gas 1. Cut any excess fat and sinew off the beef (don't worry about leaving some – it will render down in the cooking) and cut the meat into about 12 large even-sized pieces. Sprinkle with the flour, season with the allspice, salt and pepper and toss well together. Put the meat in a large casserole dish with the onion and bay leaves, pour over the port, porter, stock and 2 tablespoons of mushroom ketchup or vinegar.

Gradually bring to the boil then cover and cook in a low oven for about 2 1/2–3 hours until the meat is tender (slightly less if you're going to cool and reheat it). Turn the heat down a setting if it seems to be cooking too fast. About half an hour before the stew is due to be ready, cook the swede in boiling vegetable stock for about 15 minutes until soft. Drain well and mash roughly. Add the butter and season well with salt and freshly ground pepper.

When the meat is cooked check the seasoning, adding a little more mushroom ketchup or vinegar if you think it needs it and an extra splash of port to taste. If it's too bitter add a little tomato ketchup.

SOME GARLIC GREENS (p133) OR BRAISED CARROTS (p126), WOULD GO WELL WITH THIS. YOU COULD ALSO SERVE IT WITH BOILED OR MASHED POTATOES INSTEAD OF SWEDE.

OXTAIL IN CLARET

This is one of those epic dishes you need to start the day before, and finish the next. But it's well worth the wait. You don't have to use claret – any halfway decent red wine will do – or stout for that matter, but I like the Britishness of using Bordeaux. Drink an even better one with it.

SERVES 4–6

1 good meaty oxtail (about 1.5kg) cut into sections
40g beef dripping
2 medium onions, peeled and roughly chopped
2 carrots, peeled and sliced
2 cloves of garlic, peeled and chopped
2 tbsp plain flour plus 1 tsp for the butter paste, if needed
2 level tbsp tomato purée
$\frac{1}{4}$ tsp ground allspice
375ml inexpensive red Bordeaux or other medium to full-bodied red wine plus a little extra to finish the dish
400ml beef stock
1 stick of celery, trimmed and sliced
1 bay leaf
1 bouquet garni or a few thyme stalks tied with string
A small strip of orange rind
1 tsp butter, if needed
1–2 tbsp Cognac or Armagnac
3 tbsp finely chopped parsley
Salt and freshly ground black pepper

Soak the oxtail for 2–4 hours in salted water. Drain, cover in fresh cold water and bring to the boil. Keep at a bare simmer and skim off the froth for about 10 minutes until the froth turns white rather than a greyish brown. Drain the oxtail and leave until cool enough to handle. Preheat the oven to 150C/300F/Gas 2. Heat 25g of the beef dripping in a large casserole, large enough to take the meat in a single layer. Brown the oxtail well on all sides and set aside. Add a little more dripping then add the onion, carrots and garlic, stir and cook for a couple of minutes. Stir in the flour, tomato purée and allspice, cook for a few seconds then add the wine and stock and bring to the boil. Add the celery, bay leaf, bouquet garni and orange rind then return the meat to the pan and stir well. Bring back to

the boil then cover the stew closely with greaseproof paper, put a lid on the pan and transfer to the oven. Cook for 3$\frac{1}{2}$–4 hours checking occasionally to make sure it's not cooking too fast – the surface should barely tremble. Take the pan out of the oven, remove the paper, cool and refrigerate.

The next day, reheat the oven to 180C/350F/Gas 4. Scrape the fat off the surface of the casserole, put on the lid and heat through for about 30–40 minutes. If the sauce is too thin remove the meat, and cook the sauce fast on the top of the stove to reduce it. Strain the sauce and return it to the pan. (If it still needs thickening mash a tsp of flour with an equal amount of butter and whisk it into the casserole.) Add an extra splash (about 3 tbsp) of wine and a dash (about 1 tbsp) of Cognac if you have some. Return the meat to the pan and heat through. Season to taste with salt and black pepper. Scatter with a little parsley.

YOU DEFINITELY NEED SOMETHING TO MOP UP ALL THE RICH JUICES – MASHED POTATO OR **PARSNIP PUREE** (p129) FOR EXAMPLE. **SLOW-ROAST CARROTS** (p124) CAN COOK AT THE SAME TIME YOU REHEAT THE STEW. **BRAISED CELERY WITH FENNEL** (p123) WOULD ALSO BE GOOD.

BEEF AND CHESTNUT CASSEROLE

When my kids were small I ran a frozen food catering company called Frozen Assets, which stocked my neighbours' freezers. This recipe, which originally came from an old Good Housekeeping book, was one of the most popular recipes, despite the strange inclusion of sliced garlic sausage. Here's a slightly more sophisticated version. Oddly, I think the cooked red peppers in a jar work best in this dish but replace them with a couple of fresh peppers if you prefer, adding them after the onions.

SERVES 6

3 tbsp plain flour
1.25kg braising steak, trimmed of excess fat and cut into large cubes
4–5 tbsp olive oil
150g piece of streaky bacon, rind removed and diced, or 150g pancetta, diced
1 large onion, peeled and thinly sliced
2 cloves of garlic, peeled and crushed
1 x 400g tin premium tomatoes
150ml fresh beef stock
150ml full-bodied southern French or Spanish red wine
1 x 320g jar whole, sweet red peppers, drained and sliced
200g vacuum-packed whole chestnuts (Merchant Gourmet does very good ones)
Salt and pepper
Flat-leaf parsley to garnish

Preheat the oven to 170C/325F/Gas 3. Put the flour in a shallow dish and season with salt and pepper. Toss the beef cubes in the flour, shaking off any excess. Heat a frying pan, add 2 tbsp of the oil and fry a third to a half of the meat, browning it well on all sides. Transfer to a casserole with a slotted spoon. Repeat with the remaining meat, adding more oil as necessary. Fry the bacon lightly in the pan and add to the meat then fry the onion for 4–5 minutes until soft. Stir in the garlic and any remaining flour then add the tomatoes, stock and wine and bring to the boil. Pour the liquid over the meat, stir well, cover and cook for 3 hours until the meat is tender, checking occasionally that the casserole is not cooking too fast. 45 minutes before the end of the cooking time add the sliced red peppers and chestnuts. Check the seasoning, adding salt and pepper to taste. Scatter over a little chopped parsley before serving.

THIS IS A GOOD DISH TO SERVE WITH **BAKED POTATOES** (p118) – BUT MODESTLY-SIZED ONES PLEASE, NOT THOSE GREAT FOOTBALLS OF SPUDS. A GREEN VEGETABLE SUCH AS GREEN BEANS OR BROCCOLI WOULD BE NICE WITH IT TOO.

THREE-DAY LAMB SHANKS WITH RED WINE, ROSEMARY & GARLIC

Lamb shanks (the lower bit of the leg) lend themselves particularly well to long, slow cooking but you might think three days sounds a bit over the top. Don't be put off though. It doesn't mean it takes three days to cook, simply that the preparation is spread over three days, so you can start it on Friday to eat for Sunday lunch! And each stage is really easy.

SERVES 6 RUGBY PLAYERS

6 lamb shanks (about 2kg in total)
1 large onion, sliced
2–3 carrots, peeled and cut into strips
4 cloves of garlic, peeled and finely
   sliced
1 sprig of fresh rosemary
8 peppercorns
1 bottle of inexpensive but robust
   (12.5% or over) red wine plus an
   extra 150ml glass
2 tbsp olive oil
500ml passata
Tomato ketchup to taste
Salt and freshly ground black pepper

DAY 1
Arrange the lamb shanks in a single layer in a large deep casserole or roasting tin. Add the sliced onion, carrot strips and sliced garlic to the casserole along with the rosemary and peppercorns. Pour over the bottle of red wine, cover and leave in the fridge overnight.

DAY 2
Preheat the oven to 170C/325F/Gas 3. Remove the lamb shanks from the marinade, pat dry with kitchen paper and season with salt and freshly ground black pepper. Strain the marinade into a bowl reserving the vegetables. Heat the oil in a deep cast-iron casserole or large, lidded frying pan and brown the lamb shanks thoroughly on all sides (you'll need to do this in two batches). Set aside. Add the vegetables to the pan and fry briefly until beginning to soften. Add a few tablespoons of the marinade and de-glaze the pan, letting the liquid bubble up and scraping off any sediment with a wooden spoon. Add the passata and mix thoroughly. Put the lamb shanks back in the casserole, spoon over the vegetables and sauce and pour over the rest of the marinade. Cover with a sheet of greaseproof paper or baking parchment, then the casserole lid and cook in the preheated oven for 2 hours. Remove the lid and paper and cook for another 30 minutes. Take off the heat and cool thoroughly before covering and transferring to the fridge overnight.

DAY 3
Carefully remove any fat that has accumulated on the surface and take out the rosemary. Remove the lamb shanks and set on one side. Slowly reheat the sauce on the top of the stove. If it seems a bit thin bubble briskly to reduce until it thickens. Pour in the extra glass of wine and check the seasoning, adding salt and pepper to taste. If you think it needs a touch more sweetness add a tablespoon of tomato ketchup. When it reaches a coating consistency return the lamb shanks to the pan, cover and reheat for 30–40 minutes until completely heated through.

GOOD WITH MASHED POTATO AND **GARLICKY GREEN BEANS** (p140).

SPRING LAMB STEW WITH HERBS AND LEMON

Round about the end of March I begin to get fed up with rich dark stews and crave something lighter. This fits the bill perfectly. I'm not sure that frozen broad beans aren't actually better with this unless you're picking them straight from the garden. You want small ones anyway.

SERVES 4

450g lean lamb steaks, cubed
3 tbsp light olive or sunflower oil
1 medium onion, peeled and roughly chopped
2 medium carrots, peeled and thinly sliced
Grated rind of 1/2 a lemon
1 rounded tbsp plain flour
350ml chicken stock or stock made with 1/2 an organic chicken stock cube
125g (podded weight) small fresh or frozen broad beans
75g fresh or frozen peas
1 heaped tbsp finely chopped fresh dill
1 heaped tbsp finely chopped fresh parsley
2 tbsp crème fraîche or double cream
Salt, freshly ground black pepper and lemon juice to season

Trim any excess fat off the lamb. Heat a frying pan over a high heat for 2–3 minutes, add 1 tbsp of the oil and fry the meat quickly on all sides until lightly browned. Transfer to a casserole or saucepan. Turn the heat down, add the remaining oil and tip in the chopped onion and carrot and cook gently for about 5 minutes until beginning to soften. Add the lemon rind and flour, stir for a minute then add the stock and bring to the boil. Pour the stock and vegetables over the meat, cover and simmer over a low heat for about 45 minutes until the meat is just tender. Add the broad beans and peas, bring back to simmering point and continue to cook for about 15 minutes until the vegetables are ready. Turn off the heat and stir in the dill, parsley and crème fraîche or cream. Season with salt, pepper and a good squeeze of lemon.

THIS DISH CONTAINS ALL ITS OWN VEGETABLES BUT YOU COULD SERVE SOME SPINACH OR GREEN BEANS WITH IT IF YOU LIKE, AND RICE OR BUTTERED NEW POTATOES, I SUGGEST.

LAMB, OLIVE AND AUBERGINE STEW

I can't resist the combination of lamb and aubergines. Stews aren't generally good in hot weather but this one is.

SERVES 4

4–5 tbsp olive oil

750g shoulder of lamb, trimmed of excess fat and cubed

1 medium-sized aubergine, cubed

1 medium onion, peeled and sliced

2 large cloves of garlic, crushed

400g very ripe tomatoes, skinned and roughly chopped or 1 x 400g tin of tomatoes, roughly chopped

$1/2$ tsp cinnamon

1 tsp ground cumin

125g black olives marinated with garlic and herbs

Salt and pepper

2 heaped tbsp chopped flat-leaf parsley or coriander

Heat a large lidded frying pan or casserole, add half the oil, heat for a minute then brown the lamb cubes briefly on all sides. (You may have to do this in two batches.) Transfer the meat to a plate with a slotted spoon. Tip the cubed aubergine in the pan and stir-fry on a moderately high heat until beginning to brown, adding just enough extra oil to stop it catching. Set aside with the lamb. Turn the heat down, add the remaining oil and fry the onion for about 3–4 minutes until beginning to soften. Add the crushed garlic and tomatoes and cook for another 3–4 minutes until the tomatoes begin to break down and become jammy. Stir in the cinnamon, cumin and olives and pour in half a wine glass (about 75ml) of water. Return the meat to the pan, stir, bring to the boil then turn the heat right down, cover and simmer for $1^{1}/_{2}$ hours or until the meat is tender, stirring the stew every so often and adding a little extra water if it seems to be drying out. Season to taste with salt and pepper and stir in the parsley or coriander. Serve with couscous.

STEAMED COURGETTES, I THINK, ARE THE IDEAL VEGETABLES TO GO WITH THIS, OR YOU COULD SERVE IT WITH A ROCKET OR WATERCRESS SALAD.

GOULASH

Paprika was one of the few spices that was widely available in the '60s and '70s, hence the popularity of goulash, a dish that does not deserve to have dropped off the radar. Nowadays I prefer to use Spanish pimenton.

SERVES 4

750g pork shoulder, cut into large cubes
3 tbsp sunflower oil or other light cooking oil
2–3 medium onions (about 300–350g), peeled and finely sliced
1 large clove of garlic, peeled and crushed
2 tsp Spanish pimenton dulce (sweet pimenton) plus 1 tsp pimenton piccante (spicy) or 2–3 tsp of paprika
1 tbsp tomato purée
1 tbsp plain flour
200g can or $1/2$ a 400g tin whole or chopped tomatoes
250ml light chicken or vegetable stock made with $1/2$ an organic stock cube or 1 tsp vegetable bouillon powder
1 green pepper, quartered, de-seeded and sliced
1 red pepper, quartered, de-seeded and sliced
Salt and ground black pepper
A small carton of sour cream

Heat a large frying pan or other lidded casserole, add 2 tbsp of the oil and fry the meat on all sides. (You may have to do this in two batches, adding extra oil if necessary.) Transfer the meat to a plate with a slotted spoon. Add the remaining oil to the pan and tip in the onions. Stir and fry them for about 3–4 minutes until beginning to soften. Add the garlic, pimenton, tomato purée and flour and stir well, then return the meat to the casserole. Stir to ensure the meat is thoroughly coated then add the chopped tomatoes and stock. Bring to the boil then cover the pan, turn the heat right down to a bare simmer or transfer the pot to a low oven (150C/300F/Gas 2). Cook for 2 hours, checking from time to time that the meat is not cooking too fast. After an hour, add the sliced peppers, stir and replace the lid. Before serving check the seasoning, adding salt and pepper to taste. Stir the sour cream and spoon a little over each portion as you serve up.

PLAIN BOILED POTATOES ARE PERFECT WITH GOULASH AND **A SIMPLE LETTUCE SALAD** (p150).

MEDIAEVAL SPICED PORK WITH RED WINE AND ORANGE

The idea of putting meat and fruit together originally came from the Arab world but was very popular in mediaeval Britain. I find it irresistibly Christmassy – almost like cooking pork in mulled wine. The spicing is subtle rather than hot, the end result surprisingly sweet.

SERVES 4–6

900g pork shoulder
4–5 tbsp light olive or sunflower oil
1 large onion (about 225g), peeled and roughly chopped
2 large cloves of garlic, peeled and crushed
1 tsp finely chopped fresh rosemary leaves
1 rounded tbsp plain flour
1 tsp each of ground ginger, ground coriander and paprika
$1/2$ tsp cinnamon
1 bulb of fennel (about 225–250g), trimmed and sliced
125g organic dried apricots, cut in half
300ml full-bodied red wine
1 tbsp clear honey
Juice of half an orange (about 2 tbsp) and a thin strip of orange peel
Salt and freshly ground black pepper

Preheat the oven to 150C/300F/Gas 2. Trim the meat of excess fat and cut into large cubes. Heat 2 tbsp of the oil in a frying pan and quickly sear the meat on both sides (do this in two batches so you can keep the meat in a single layer, add an extra spoonful of oil if you need to.) Remove to a large casserole. Add the remaining oil to the frying pan and fry the onion for 3–4 minutes without browning until beginning to soften. Add the crushed garlic and rosemary, cook for a minute, then add the flour and the dry spices and stir. Add the sliced fennel, apricots, wine, honey, orange juice and peel, stir thoroughly and bring to the boil. Pour over the pork, cover and transfer to a low oven. Cook for about $1/2$–2 hours, until the pork is tender, stirring it halfway through. Check the seasoning, adding plenty of freshly ground black pepper and a little salt. Remove the orange peel. Serve with buttered couscous.

WITH ALL THE FRUIT AND VEGETABLES IN THE STEW, I'M NOT SURE YOU NEED MORE THAN **A SIMPLE LETTUCE SALAD** (p150).

WEST COUNTRY CHICKEN CASSEROLE WITH CIDER, APPLE AND CELERY

A homely, comforting and very English tasting casserole. Do try and find some proper 'dirty celery' with some soil still clinging to the stalks. It has so much more flavour.

SERVES 4

2 level tbsp plain flour
4 boneless (but not skinless) chicken
   breasts
3 tbsp light olive oil
25g butter
1 large onion (about 175g), peeled,
   halved and sliced
1 large carrot (about 125g), peeled,
   cut lengthways and sliced
2–3 sticks of 'dirty' celery, washed,
   trimmed and sliced
$1/2$ tsp fresh thyme
175ml ready-made fresh chicken
   stock
175ml dry cider
1 large or 2 smaller Cox or Blenheim
   apples (about 150g) peeled and
   sliced
Salt and freshly ground black pepper
Chives to decorate

Put the flour in a shallow bowl and season with salt and pepper. Pat the chicken breasts dry with kitchen paper then coat them thoroughly in the seasoned flour, shaking off any excess. Heat a large, deep, lidded frying pan or casserole for a couple of minutes over a moderately high heat. Add 1 tbsp of oil, then, when that is hot, half the butter. Place the chicken breasts in the pan, skin-side downwards and fry for 2–3 minutes until the skin is nicely browned. Turn the breasts over, turn the heat down and fry the other side for about $1^1/2$ minutes. Remove the chicken breasts to a plate, discard the fat in the pan and wipe it clean.

Return the pan to a moderate heat and add the remaining oil and butter. Add the onion, carrot and celery, stir well, cover the pan and cook for 5 minutes until the vegetables are beginning to soften. Stir in the thyme and any leftover flour and stir. Add the chicken stock and cider, bring to the boil and add the sliced apples. Turn the heat down and return the chicken pieces to the pan, spooning the vegetables over them. Replace the lid and cook at a gentle simmer for about 35–40 minutes, stirring the vegetables occasionally to stop them sticking and turning the chicken breasts over halfway through. Add a little extra cider or chicken stock if needed. Check the seasoning, adding extra salt or pepper to taste. Serve the chicken on warm plates and top with a few scissor-snipped chives.

SERVE WITH BOILED BABY SALAD POTATOES TOSSED WITH BUTTER AND PARSLEY AND SOME LIGHTLY STEAMED OR MICROWAVED BROCCOLI.

CHICKEN CHASSEUR

One of those forgotten French dishes – for no very good reason – Chicken Chasseur is remarkably tasty. Maybe it's because the original sauce is based on a battery of cheffy sauces – demi-glace that is based on Sauce Espagnole, which, in turn, is based on a classic brown stock. But you can use any good stock or even a can of consommé. Very '70s!

SERVES 4

2–4 tbsp light olive oil or sunflower oil
4 chicken quarters
1 medium onion, finely chopped
1 large clove of garlic, finely chopped
150ml white wine
1 heaped tbsp tomato purée
300ml rich savoury stock – e.g. jellied turkey, duck or chicken stock or some leftover jellied meat juices (skimmed of fat) or a 295g tin of condensed beef consommé or a mixture of these
2–3 tbsp Madeira
20g butter
250g button mushrooms, wiped, halved or quartered
1 tbsp butter paste (optional – see method)
Freshly ground pepper and salt if needed
2 tbsp finely chopped fresh parsley

Preheat the oven to 180C/350F/Gas 4. Heat a large deep frying pan, add the oil and fry the chicken pieces on both sides until nicely browned. Transfer to a casserole large enough to take the chicken in a single layer. Pour away half the fat remaining in the pan (or discard altogether if it has got at all burnt, wipe the pan and add another 2 tbsp of oil). Add the finely chopped onion to the pan and cook slowly until soft and beginning to colour (about 3–4 minutes). Stir in the garlic and cook for a minute then pour in the wine, bubble up and reduce by half. Stir in the tomato purée then add the stock or consommé and Madeira. Bring to the boil, cook for a minute then strain the sauce over the chicken pieces. Put a lid on the casserole and transfer to the oven for 20 minutes. Wipe the frying pan clean again, put back on the heat and add the butter.

Fry the mushrooms for about 3–4 minutes till any liquid has evaporated and they are lightly browned. Add the mushrooms to the casserole and stir them into the sauce. Leave off the casserole lid and return the chicken to the oven for another 15–20 minutes until cooked. Transfer the chicken pieces to a warm plate and bubble up the sauce for a few minutes to reduce. (You can at this point, if you prefer a slightly thicker sauce, whisk in a little butter paste made by mashing a tablespoon of soft butter with an equal quantity of flour.) Season the sauce with freshly ground black pepper and salt, if you need it (unlikely with a commercial stock) and stir in the parsley. Divide the chicken between individual plates and spoon over the sauce.

GOOD WITH MASH OR SAUTE POTATOES (p116) AND SOME GREEN BEANS.

BRAISED CHICKEN WITH BACON AND CHICORY

A slight adaptation of a fantastic Simon Hopkinson recipe I still have on a yellowing piece of paper torn out of the Independent. *It was subsequently published in his book* Gammon and Spinach.

SERVES 4

2 tbsp plain flour
8 chicken thighs or 4 chicken legs
  (about 1kg in total)
2 tbsp olive or sunflower oil
40g butter
175g piece of dry-cured smoked
  streaky bacon, rinded and 2 small
  packs (about 160g) pancetta cubetti
1 medium onion, peeled and finely
  chopped
8 small endive (chicory) heads or 4
  larger ones, trimmed and halved
Juice of 2 lemons (plus, optionally, a
couple of the empty lemon halves)
150ml dry white wine
75ml chicken stock
2 heaped tbsp flat-leaf parsley
Salt and pepper

Preheat the oven to 180C/350F/Gas 4. Put the flour in a shallow dish and season with salt and pepper. Dust the chicken pieces with the flour, ensuring they are evenly coated and shake off any excess. Heat a large frying pan for a couple of minutes then add 1 tablespoon of oil and half the butter. Fry the chicken pieces on all sides until golden brown and transfer to a large roasting tin or baking dish big enough to take the chicken and chicory in a single layer. Tip the bacon into the frying pan, stir, then add the onion and fry for about 3 minutes until beginning to soften. Remove with a slotted spoon and add to the chicken. Pour off the fat if it has become at all discoloured, wipe the pan and add the remaining oil and butter. Brown the chicory heads lightly on all sides and add to the chicken. Pour the lemon juice into the pan over a low heat working any nice crusty bits off the side and pour over the chicken. (Tuck in a couple of the empty lemon halves to accentuate the lemon flavour, if your lemons don't have much juice.) Pour the wine and chicken stock in the pan, bubble up and reduce by half then pour over the chicken. Cover the chicken lightly with foil, transfer to the oven and cook for 30 minutes then remove the foil and cook for another 20–25 minutes until the chicken and chicory are both brown and sticky. Stir the parsley into the pan juices just before serving.

CHICORY DOES DUTY FOR POTATOES HERE BUT YOU COULD SERVE A FEW NEW POTATOES WITH THIS IF YOU'RE A POTATO ADDICT. **BRAISED CARROTS** (p126) WOULD ALSO MAKE A GOOD ACCOMPANIMENT.

CHICKEN IN A (CROCK) POT WITH AIOLI

I'm completely won over to the virtues of the new generation of slow cookers. They help control a dish like this, where the liquid barely needs to tremble, perfectly. It will also help to create a fantastic jellied stock – if you have any leftover. Obviously the aioli is not terribly British but I find the dish a little bland without it.

SERVES 4

A medium-sized chicken (about 1.25kg)
1 medium-sized onion, peeled and cut into 8
2–3 carrots, peeled and sliced
1 small or $1/2$ larger bulb of fennel
250g baby new potatoes (if you have room in the pot, otherwise cook them separately)
About 1 litre light chicken stock or vegetable stock made with 1 tbsp vegetable bouillon powder
1 bay leaf
6–8 peppercorns
2 tbsp finely chopped parsley

Put the chicken in a large pot with the onions, carrots, fennel and potatoes, if using, pour in the stock and enough water to cover and bring to the boil over a moderate heat. (This will take about 20-25 minutes). Skim off any froth and add the bay leaf and peppercorns. Turn the heat down to a bare simmer and cook for 50 minutes to an hour or until the chicken is tender. Alternatively transfer the chicken and vegetables to a slow cooker and pour in just enough stock to cover leaving about 2cm free at the top of the pot. Follow the instructions in the leaflet that will probably recommend you to cook the chicken for something like 6-8 hours. Remove the chicken from the cooking liquid and let it rest in a warm place for 10-15 minutes before carving. Serve the chicken and vegetables in large soup bowls with plenty of liquor, a good dollop of aioli and a scattering of parsley.

AIOLI

Aioli is undoubtedly better if you make it by hand but it's a lot easier by machine. Either way though, make the garlic paste with a pestle and mortar.

2–3 large cloves of garlic, peeled and roughly chopped
$1/2$ tsp coarse sea salt
1 large fresh egg yolk, at room temperature
150ml light olive oil
$1/4$ tsp wine vinegar
Freshly ground black pepper

Put the garlic in a mortar with the salt and pound until you have a smooth paste. (If you are going to make the aioli in a food processor transfer the garlic at this point.) Add the egg yolk and work it in. Pour the oil in a jug then gradually add it drop by drop to the egg and garlic mixture, pounding away with the pestle all the time. Once the mixture thickens, add a few drops of vinegar and increase the speed you add the oil to a steady fine stream. Once all the oil has been incorporated add 1–2 teaspoons of the chicken cooking liquid, $1/2$ a teaspoon at a time to lighten and loosen the mixture.

I'M NOT SURE YOU NEED ANY EXTRA VEGETABLES WITH THIS BUT YOU COULD SERVE SOME LIGHTLY STEAMED BROCCOLI AND SOME EXTRA NEW POTATOES.

BOILED BACON WITH BROAD BEANS AND PARSLEY SAUCE

When you taste this you'll wonder why you don't eat dishes like this more often. Simple, delicious English food. If you forget to soak the bacon just cover it with cold water, bring to the boil and discard the water.

SERVES 4–6

1.5kg piece smoked collar of bacon or gammon, soaked overnight in cold water
1 small onion, peeled and quartered
2 carrots, peeled and cut into 3 or 4 pieces
1 stick of celery, washed, trimmed and cut into 3 pieces
A few peppercorns

FOR THE SAUCE

1 small onion, peeled and halved
1 bay leaf
350ml whole or semi-skimmed milk
25g butter
25g plain flour
400g (podded weight) fresh or frozen broad beans
A small bunch or pack of parsley (about 20g), destalked and finely chopped
Salt and freshly ground black pepper

Drain the bacon, put in a large saucepan and cover with fresh, cold water. Bring slowly to the boil and skim off any froth. Tuck the vegetables round the sides, add the peppercorns, bring back to the boil then turn down the heat and simmer very slowly, so that bubbles just break on the surface, for about 2 hours. About an hour before the bacon is due to be ready put an onion and bay leaf in a small pan and pour over the milk. Heat slowly until the milk is almost boiling then take off the heat, cover and set aside for half an hour.

Cook the broad beans lightly (about 5 minutes) and drain. (If the beans you have used are quite large, and you have the patience, you can slip off their skins after you've boiled them.)

Pass the milk through a sieve into a jug. Heat the butter gently in a non-stick pan, stir in the flour and cook for a few seconds. Pour in the warm milk in one go, whisking as you pour with a wire whisk. It should rapidly thicken. Replace over a low heat and continue to simmer for a few minutes, adding a couple of tablespoons of the ham cooking liquid to get a nice light texture. Tip in the drained broad beans and stir in the parsley. Check the seasoning adding salt and pepper to taste. Carve the ham in thick slices and serve with the broad beans and parsley sauce.

NEW OR BOILED POTATOES IN THEIR SKINS ARE PERFECT WITH THIS. YOU COULD ALSO SERVE THE CARROTS YOU BOILED WITH THE HAM OR COOK SOME EXTRA ONES TO GO WITH THE DISH.

PIES & BAKES

INDIVIDUAL SHEPHERD'S PIES

I've never been convinced of the virtue of making shepherd's pie from leftover meat, but leftover gravy is another matter. If you have some do use it. And you can add in a small amount of finely chopped cooked meat, especially if it's rare but use fresh meat too. You can of course make this as a single pie in which case increase the cooking time to 30–35 minutes. But giving everyone their own pie makes it seem more of a treat. Or just make a supply to keep in the freezer.

SERVES 4

3 tbsp light olive or sunflower oil
250g lean minced lamb
250g lean minced beef
1 medium onion, peeled and finely
   chopped
1 clove of garlic, peeled and crushed
$\frac{1}{2}$ tsp dried oregano or herbes de
   Provence
1 level tbsp tomato purée
1 tsp plain flour (if using stock rather
   than gravy)
225ml leftover or shop-bought gravy
   or 1 tsp Bovril mixed with 225ml
   boiling water
Salt and freshly ground black pepper

FOR THE POTATO TOPPING
500g King Edward or other good
   boiling potatoes, peeled and cut
   into even-sized pieces (halves or
   quarters depending on size)
15g soft butter
A splash of warm milk (about 2 tbsp)
Salt and pepper

Heat a large frying pan, add 1 tbsp of the oil and fry the lamb until lightly browned. Remove the meat with a slotted spoon, letting the fat run back into the pan then discard the fat. Add the beef to the pan, brown it and drain off the fat in a similar way. Add the remaining oil and fry the onion over a low heat for about 5 minutes until soft. Stir in the crushed garlic, oregano and tomato purée and cook for a few seconds. If you're using leftover or shop-bought gravy tip it in. If you don't have any, stir in 1 tsp of plain flour then add the beef or Bovril stock. Bring to the boil and simmer till thick. Tip the mince back in the pan, bring back to simmering point then turn the heat right down and leave on a low heat for about 20 minutes. Set aside and leave to cool. (You can make this part of the recipe in advance.)

Put the potatoes in a saucepan, cover with cold water and bring to the boil. Cook for about 20 minutes until you can stick the point of a knife in them easily. Drain the potatoes, return them to the pan and cut them up roughly with a knife. Mash them thoroughly with a potato masher or fork. Beat in the butter and warm milk. Season with salt and pepper. Preheat the oven to 200C/400F/Gas 6. Divide the meat between 4 small individual pie dishes and spread the potato evenly over the top, roughing up the surface with the prongs of a fork. Place the pies on a baking tray and bake for 20–25 minutes until the tops are nice and crispy.

PEAS ARE TRADITIONAL WITH SHEPHERD'S PIE BUT OTHER VEGETABLES WOULD BE EQUALLY NICE. CARROTS, GREEN OR RUNNER BEANS, SPROUTS.... OR TRY THE **NOT-AT-ALL-BORING PEAS AND CARROTS** (p127)

DOUBLE DUCK PIE

A great recipe that can be made from scratch but which is even better made with leftovers from a rich, dark meaty stew.

SERVES 3–4

2 duck legs or 250–300g cooked duck meat
A small tin of confit de canard (2 legs)
A portion (about 300g) of leftover beef or oxtail stew (see p44 or p46) – optional but good or 250ml Five Spice Onion Gravy (see right for recipe)
Salt, pepper, ground five spice and Worcestershire sauce to taste

FOR THE POTATO TOPPING
800g potatoes, peeled and quartered
25g butter
50–75ml warm milk
Salt and pepper

You will need a medium-sized cast-iron baking dish or roasting tin with a capacity of 1.5 litres.

Preheat the oven to 200C/400F/Gas 6. Trim the excess fat off the duck legs and sprinkle the skin with a little five spice powder. Put in a lightly greased roasting tin and cook for 15 minutes. Pour off the fat and return the duck to the oven and cook for another 15 minutes. Pour off the fat again and add the two duck confit legs, (having scraped as much of the fat off them as possible) and cook for another 10–15 minutes. Remove the duck pieces from the tin, remove the skin and pull off and shred the meat.

Pour off the rest of the fat from the roasting tin (keeping it for roasting potatoes) and tip the shredded duck meat back in the tin together with the leftover stew, if using. (Or make up a batch of onion gravy following the recipe below and add that to the duck meat.) Put the roasting tin on the hob, bring the mixture to the boil and simmer for 3–4 minutes. Check the seasoning, adding salt, pepper and a little more five spice or a few drops of Worcestershire sauce, if you think it

needs it, and transfer to an ovenproof dish. While the duck is cooking boil the potatoes until tender (about 20–25 minutes). Cut them up and mash them, then add in the butter and warm milk and beat well. Season with salt and pepper. Spread the mashed potato evenly over the duck mixture. Bake the pie for about 30–35 minutes until the top is crusted and brown.

FIVE SPICE ONION GRAVY
Heat a tablespoon of oil in a saucepan, add a small slice of butter (about 15g) and tip in a finely sliced onion. Stir and cook over a moderate heat for about 6–7 minutes until soft and beginning to brown. Stir in a small pinch of five spice powder and 1 tbsp of plain flour then add 225ml of beef stock or stock made with 225ml boiling water and 1 tsp Bovril. Bring to the boil, turn the heat down and simmer for 5–10 minutes until thick. Season to taste with a little salt and freshly ground black pepper.

YOU COULD SERVE THIS WITH PEAS AND CARROTS LIKE ANY COTTAGE PIE BUT I PARTICULARLY LIKE IT WITH **GARLICKY GREEN BEANS** (p140). YOU COULD ALSO VARY THE TOPPING BY SUBSTITUTING **PARSNIP PUREE** (p129) FOR THE POTATO.

ANGLO-INDIAN SHEPHERD'S PIE

Curried meat has had a firm place in the British meat repertoire since the days of the Raj and, together with this spicy potato topping, adds an appealing twist to a shepherd's pie.

SERVES 4

450g beef or lamb mince, or a mixture
   of the two
1 tbsp light olive or sunflower oil
1 heaped tbsp tomato purée
2 large cloves of garlic, peeled and
   crushed
2–3 tsp medium hot curry paste
1 x 200g or $\frac{1}{2}$ a 400g tin chopped or
   whole tomatoes
75g frozen peas
3 heaped tbsp finely chopped
   coriander

FOR THE MASH

About 750g old potatoes, peeled
   and halved or quartered, depending
   on size
$\frac{1}{4}$ tsp ground turmeric (optional)
1 clove of garlic, crushed with $\frac{1}{2}$ tsp
   sea salt
2–3 tbsp low-fat yoghurt
Freshly ground black pepper

Heat a large frying pan over a moderately high heat for a couple of minutes. Add the oil, swirl round the pan then tip in the mince spreading it around the pan. Fry until beginning to brown then turn it over with a wooden spoon or spatula. Keep frying until all the mince is browned (about $1\frac{1}{2}$–2 minutes). Tip the pan away from you, scoop out the mince onto a large plate and discard the fat that has accumulated in the pan. Turn down the heat a little and return all the meat to the pan without any further oil. Add the tomato purée, stir into the meat until it is well distributed, stirring it all the time. Add the garlic, curry paste and tinned tomatoes (breaking them up with a fork if they are whole).

Season with salt and pepper, bring to a simmer then turn the heat right down and leave to cook gently while you cook the potatoes (about 20–25 minutes). Take off the heat and stir in the peas and chopped coriander. Tip the mince into a lightly oiled shallow ovenproof dish and turn the oven on to 200C/400F/Gas 6.

Put the potatoes in a large saucepan with cold water to cover. Bring to the boil, add salt then cook for about 15–20 minutes until you can stick a knife into the pieces without any resistance. Drain the potatoes in a colander or sieve, return to the pan and mash with a fork or potato masher until smooth and lump-free. Sprinkle over the turmeric, add the yoghurt and crushed garlic and mash again. Spread the mashed potato evenly over the mince, roughing up the surface with a fork. Bake the pie for 30–35 minutes until the top is nice and brown.

SOME LIGHTLY SPICED CARROTS OR CAULIFLOWER WOULD BE GOOD WITH THIS. ADD A GOOD PINCH OF GROUND CORIANDER OR CUMIN SEEDS TO THE **BRAISED CARROTS** (p126) OR UP THE SPICING ON THE **FRIED CAULIFLOWER WITH ONION** (p135).

GARDENER'S PIE

A cottage pie for vegetable lovers. A good dish to serve to kids as most of the vegetables are cunningly concealed in the topping.

SERVES 4

3 tbsp light olive or sunflower oil
500g lean minced pork
1 medium onion, peeled and finely chopped
1 stick of celery, trimmed and finely chopped
1 clove of garlic, peeled and crushed
$\frac{1}{2}$ tsp dried oregano or herbes de Provence
1 tbsp tomato purée
3–4 medium tomatoes, skinned and roughly chopped or 150g good quality passata
1 tsp Marmite mixed with 150ml boiling water
Salt and freshly ground black pepper

FOR THE TOPPING
2 medium sized potatoes, peeled and halved (about 350g)
1 medium-sized parsnip (about 150g)
1 medium-sized carrot (about 100g)
1 medium-sized leek (about 125g)
3 tbsp light olive or sunflower oil
25g grated, mature Cheddar
Salt and freshly ground black pepper

Heat a large frying pan, add 1 tbsp of the oil and fry the meat until browned all over. Remove the meat with a slotted spoon, set aside and pour off the fat. Add the remaining oil and fry the onion and celery over a low heat for about 5 minutes until soft. Stir in the crushed garlic, oregano and tomato purée, cook for a few seconds then add the tomatoes or passata, turn up the heat and cook for about 5 minutes until the tomatoes have broken down and reduced to a thick sauce. Stir in the Marmite stock and bring to the boil. Tip the mince back in the pan, bring back to the boil then turn the heat right down and leave on a very low heat while you prepare the vegetable topping.

Cover the potatoes with cold water, bring to the boil and cook for 10 minutes. Drain and leave until cool enough to handle. Peel and coarsely grate the parsnips and carrot and clean and finely slice the leek. Coarsely grate the potatoes. Heat the oil in a frying pan or wok and tip in the leeks. Stir-fry for a minute then add the remaining vegetables and stir-fry for a couple of minutes mixing the vegetables together well. Take off the heat and season generously with salt and pepper.

Heat the oven to 190C/375F/Gas 6. Put the mince in a lightly greased shallow baking dish and cover with the vegetables. Sprinkle over the cheese. Bake for 30–35 minutes until the top is brown and crispy. (If you make the pie ahead and are reheating it from cold increase the cooking time to 45–50 minutes).

AS YOU'VE USED VIRTUALLY EVERY VEG IN THE BOOK FOR THIS I'M NOT SURE YOU NEED ANY MORE BUT SOME RUNNER BEANS WOULD BE NICE.

STEAK & KIDNEY AND MUSHROOM PIE

If you usually eat out all the time this is the kind of homey dish to serve friends for Sunday lunch. (If you don't like kidneys leave them out and increase the amount of steak and mushrooms.)

SERVES 6

750g lean braising steak
250g ox kidney
5–6 tbsp olive or sunflower oil
1 large onion, peeled and sliced
1 rounded tbsp plain flour, seasoned
  with salt and pepper
350ml fresh beef stock or stock made
  with an organic beef stock cube
2 tbsp tomato ketchup
1–1$\frac{1}{2}$ tsp Worcestershire sauce
1-1$\frac{1}{2}$ tsp mushroom ketchup
250g large flat mushrooms
Sea salt and freshly ground black
  pepper
A 375g pack frozen puff pastry,
  thawed
1 medium egg

Trim any excess fat off the steak and remove the core from the kidney. Cut the meats into fairly large pieces and dip them in seasoned flour. Heat 3 tbsp of the oil in a frying pan and fry the cubed meat in batches until well browned, adding extra oil as necessary. Transfer each batch to a large casserole as you go. Add a couple more tablespoons of oil to the pan and cook the onion slowly for about 10 minutes until soft. Stir in the flour and cook for a minute. Add the stock, scraping all the yummy caramelised bits off the pan and then add the tomato ketchup, Worcestershire sauce and mushroom ketchup. Bring to the boil and simmer for a couple of minutes. Pour over the beef, stir and check the seasoning, adding salt, pepper and extra ketchup or Worcestershire sauce to taste.

Cover and cook over a low heat for 2 hours or until tender, stirring occasionally. Wipe and slice the mushrooms and add them for the last 15 minutes of the cooking time. Transfer into a large pie dish and set aside until completely cold (2–3 hours). Roll out the pastry quite thickly to fit the top of your pie dish leaving some pastry over for decoration. Cut long strips of pastry the width of the pie dish rim, dampen them with water and arrange round the rim of the dish. Dampen the top edge, carefully lower the pastry lid into place then cut off any overhanging edges. Crimp the edge of the pie and cut a slit in the centre of the pastry lid. Decorate the pie with pastry flowers, leaves, stars... whatever takes your fancy. Just before baking brush the pastry with beaten egg. Heat the oven to 220C/425F/Gas 7 and bake for 20 minutes then turn the heat down to 190C/375F/Gas 5 and bake for 25–30 minutes more until the pastry is well browned and the juices are beginning to bubble under the pie crust.

YOU COULD SERVE THIS SIMPLY WITH MASH AND GREEN BEANS OR, MORE IMPRESSIVELY, WITH A **PARSNIP PUREE** (p129) AND **BRAISED RED CABBAGE** (p134).

CORNISH PASTY PIE

You might not be convinced of the virtues of making your own Cornish pasties given the number of pasty shops nowadays, but I promise you that the taste of this freshly baked pie and the smell coming from the oven as it cooks will make you change your mind. I've made it as a pie as it's much easier than trying to cram the filling into individual pasties (and also less fattening...). Do use good quality beef for it – the traditional skirt is perfect. And don't be tempted to put the vegetables and meat through a food processor. They really are better chopped by hand.

SERVES 4–6

400–425g beef skirt or lean braising beef, trimmed of fat
1 tbsp Worcestershire sauce
Half a small swede, peeled (about 225g)
450g waxy potatoes, peeled (e.g. Desirée)
2 medium-sized onions, peeled (about 225g)
1 rounded tsp sea salt
1 rounded tsp white or black peppercorns, freshly ground

FOR THE PASTRY
250g plain flour
110g block margarine (e.g. Stork) or butter
75g Cookeen or other vegetable shortening
A good pinch of salt
4–5 tbsp iced water
1 medium egg lightly beaten

You will need a lightly greased shallow round pie dish or deep flan dish about 24–26cm in diameter.

Measure out the margarine or butter and lard, wrap each piece in foil and place in the freezer to harden for at least half an hour. Cut the beef into very small cubes, put in a large bowl and mix with the Worcestershire sauce. Cut the swede into similar sized cubes, quarter and finely slice the potatoes, and finely chop the onion. Add the vegetables to the meat, season well with salt and pepper and mix well.

To make the pastry measure the flour into a bowl and coarsely grate in the semi-frozen margarine and vegetable shortening, holding the foil-covered end and dipping them in the flour as you go to stop the fat sticking to the grater. Cut the grated fat into the flour until it resembles coarse breadcrumbs then sprinkle over 4 tbsp of the iced water. Work in the liquid with a flat-bladed knife, adding enough extra liquid to enable you to pull the mixture together into a ball. Put the pastry onto a floured board, shape it into a flat disc then place in a plastic bag and chill it in the fridge for half an hour.

Preheat the oven to 200C/400F/Gas 6. Grease the inside of the pie dish lightly with margarine or butter, tip the filling into it and pack it down well. Moisten the rim of the pie dish with water. Roll out the pastry to a circle slightly wider than the diameter of the dish and carefully lay it over the meat mixture. Press it down lightly inside the rim and trim off any overhanging pieces with a sharp knife. Cut a slit in the centre of the pie and brush the surface with the beaten egg. Decorate the pie with the trimmings if you feel inspired to. Bake the pie for 30 minutes then turn the heat down to 180C/350F/Gas 4 and bake another 30 minutes. Remove from the oven and cool for at least 30 minutes. Serve warm or at room temperature.

THERE ARE ALREADY MORE VEGETABLES THAN MEAT IN THIS PIE BUT I SUGGEST YOU SERVE IT WITH A SIMPLE GREEN OR MIXED SALAD.

CUMBERLAND SAUSAGE AND ONION SLICE

Essentially an outsize sausage roll, this incredibly easy pie makes a brilliant meal for a large family gathering. I've kept it completely plain to give it maximum appeal to picky eaters but you can ring the changes with different types of sausage, or by adding chopped apple, chopped parsley or both. When you're using sausage meat, by the way, it's always worth buying sausages and skinning them rather than buying sausage meat as it is very rarely of equal quality.

SERVES 8

2 x 375g packs ready-rolled puff pastry
2 tbsp light olive or sunflower oil
1 large mild onion or 2 smaller ones – about 300–325g in total, peeled and finely chopped
750g Cumberland or other premium quality traditional sausages (about 10 thick sausages)
40g fresh breadcrumbs made from a traditional white loaf
$1/4$ tsp ground white pepper
1 medium egg, lightly beaten
A little flour for rolling out the pastry

Take the packs of pastry out of the fridge for 20 minutes before you unroll them. Heat the oil in a large frying pan and cook the onion gently for about 5–6 minutes until soft and beginning to brown. Set aside to cool. Skin the sausages by making a small cut in the skin and peeling it off. Once the onions are cool mix them with the sausage and breadcrumbs and season with white pepper.

Preheat the oven to 220C/425F/Gas 7. Unroll one of the packs of pastry and lay on a lightly oiled non-stick baking tray. Spoon the filling over the top, leaving a border round the edge. Brush a little beaten egg round the border. Unroll the other piece of pastry and roll it out a little on a floured board to make it large enough to cover the filling. Lay it over the pie and lightly press down the edges on the border, trying not to stretch it too much. Trim off any overlapping edges and indent the edges of the pie at regular intervals with the back of a knife.

Brush the surface of the pie with beaten egg and make 3 small slits across the middle to allow steam to escape. Bake the pie in the pre-heated oven for 20 minutes then turn the heat down to 190C/375F/Gas 5 and bake for a further 35–40 minutes until the pie is nicely browned. Remove the pie from the oven and cool for 20 minutes before eating it (it just tastes better that way!). You could serve some apple sauce alongside for those who want it.

UP TO YOU WHETHER YOU SERVE POTATOES WITH THIS – YOU DON'T REALLY NEED THEM BUT A FEW NEW POTATOES WOULD BE NICE. OTHERWISE TAKE YOUR PICK FROM PEAS, BEANS, CABBAGE, CARROTS, CAULIFLOWER – I'D SUGGEST AT LEAST TWO.

RABBIT, BACON AND TEWKESBURY MUSTARD PIE

There's something wonderfully nostalgic about a rabbit pie even if you weren't brought up on them. Good hot, but even better, in my humble opinion, cold. The perfect pie to take on a picnic.

SERVES 6

4–5 tbsp light olive oil or sunflower oil
100g smoked bacon lardoons, or smoked streaky bacon roughly chopped
1 rabbit, jointed
250ml dry white wine
1 medium onion
1–2 carrots
1 tsp finely chopped fresh thyme
1 bay leaf
1 tbsp plain flour
500ml chicken or light vegetable stock
1 level tbsp Tewkesbury mustard
125g chestnut mushrooms
3 tbsp finely chopped parsley
Salt and freshly ground black pepper

FOR THE PASTRY
300g unbleached white flour
1/4 tsp sea salt
125g butter, chilled and cut into small cubes
75g chilled Cookeen or other vegetable shortening cut into small cubes
3 tbsp iced water
1 medium egg, lightly beaten

You will need a lightly greased shallow round pie dish or deep flan dish 24–26cm in diameter.

Heat 2 tablespoons of the oil and fry the lardons for 2–3 minutes until lightly browned. Scoop out with a slotted spoon and transfer to a deep casserole. Brown the rabbit pieces lightly on all sides and transfer to the casserole. Pour the wine into the pan and bubble up for a minute. Pour over the rabbit. Wipe the pan, replace over a medium heat and add the remaining oil. Fry the onion and carrot until beginning to soften (about 5–6 minutes). Add the thyme and stir in the flour then gradually add the stock. Pour over the rabbit and bacon, add a bay leaf and bring to the boil. Cover closely with greaseproof paper and a lid, then turn the heat right down and leave to simmer for 50–60 minutes or until tender.

While the rabbit is cooking make the pastry. Place the flour and salt in a large bowl and add the cubes of butter and Cookeen. Cut the fat into the flour then rub it in with your fingertips until it looks like coarse breadcrumbs. Sprinkle over the iced water and work it in with a flat-bladed knife, pulling the mixture together as you go. Use your hand to pull it together into a ball, then shape the pastry into a flat disc. (You can also make this in a food processor.) Cover with clingfilm and refrigerate for 30 minutes.

Once the rabbit is cooked remove the pieces from the pan and strip the meat off the bones, leaving it in fairly large chunks. Reduce the sauce by about half, until thickened, then take off the heat and add the sliced mushrooms, parsley and mustard. Add the rabbit back to the pan, stir well, check the seasoning, adding salt and pepper to taste, and leave to cool.

When the filling is cold, heat the oven to 200C/400F/Gas 6. Spoon the filling into the pie dish. Roll out the pastry quite thickly to a circle slightly larger than the width of the dish. Carefully lower it over the filling. Using a pastry brush, moisten the rim of the dish under the pastry with beaten egg then press the edges down and trim off the excess pastry round the edges. Cut a slit in the middle of the pie. To decorate the pie, press the remaining scraps of pastry together then roll it out and cut rabbit's faces or any other shapes you like from it. Brush the pie with beaten egg then decorate it, glazing the decorations with more beaten egg. Bake the pie for 35–40 minutes until the pastry is golden brown.

SERVE HOT WITH BUTTERED NEW POTATOES AND **NOT-AT-ALL-BORING PEAS AND CARROTS** (p127) OR COLD WITH A SIMPLE GREEN SALAD.

EXTRA-QUICK CHICKEN, LEEK AND TARRAGON PIE WITH DORSET BUTTER PUFF PASTRY

If you fancy a homemade pie, but haven't time to cool the filling before you put on the pastry lid, here's an easy shortcut. It also has the virtue of keeping the pastry beautifully crisp. Look out for Dorset Butter Puff Pastry which has a fantastic flavour. You can buy it online or from specialist shops.

1 pack ready-rolled Dorset Butter Puff Pastry or other puff pastry
1 egg, beaten
1 tbsp light olive or sunflower oil
50g butter
4 skinless, boneless chicken breasts (about 550–600g) cut into chunky slices
1 thick gammon steak (about 250g), fat removed and cut into cubes
175ml Chardonnay or other full-bodied dry white wine
3 tbsp finely chopped fresh tarragon
2 level tbsp plain flour
1 large leek (about 250g) washed, trimmed and finely sliced
300ml whole (as opposed to semi-skimmed) organic milk
300g frozen peas
2 tbsp crème fraîche or double cream (optional)
Sea salt and freshly ground pepper

Pre heat the oven to 200C/400F/ Gas 6. Unroll the pastry and cut into 6 rectangles. Lay on a lightly greased baking sheet, brush with beaten egg and prick with a fork. Bake for 15 minutes then turn the heat down to 180C/350F/ Gas 4 and continue to cook for another 5–10 minutes until well browned (or follow the timings and temperatures on the pack). Meanwhile, heat the oil and half the butter in a large frying pan and fry the chicken and gammon pieces until lightly coloured. (You may need to do this in two batches.) Pour over the wine and cook over a moderate heat until the liquid has reduced by two thirds (about 5–7 minutes). Stir in the fresh tarragon. Melt the remaining butter in a non-stick lidded saucepan, add the sliced leek, stir, cover and cook gently for about 5 minutes until it is soft. Stir in the flour and cook for a few seconds. Add the milk gradually, stirring continuously and cook over a low heat until the sauce has thickened (about 5 minutes). Tip the chicken, gammon and wine and the frozen peas into the sauce, stir and simmer over a low heat for about 10 minutes. Check the seasoning of the pie 'filling', adding salt and pepper to taste. Stir in a spoonful or two of crème fraîche or double cream if you feel especially indulgent. Divide the chicken between six plates and arrange a slice of pastry over the top of each.

STEAMED BROCCOLI AND ASPARAGUS ARE BOTH EXCELLENT WITH THIS. YOU DON'T REALLY NEED POTATOES BUT BUTTERED NEW POTATOES WITH PARSLEY AND CHIVES WOULD GO WELL.

PARMESAN-CRUSTED CHICKEN
WITH ROAST TOMATOES

This is a slight adaptation of a Robert Carrier recipe that I've been using for years and which is equally good for a family supper or having friends round. You can prepare the chicken in advance and keep it in the fridge for a few hours, leaving you with minimal last minute work.

SERVES 6

75g fresh breadcrumbs (see method below)
40g freshly grated Parmesan
1 large egg
2 tbsp milk
3 tbsp plain flour
6 evenly sized skinless, boneless chicken breasts – about 900g in total
4 tbsp olive oil
60g butter
6 tomatoes, halved
Salt and freshly ground black pepper

Preheat the oven to 200C/400F/Gas 6. To make fresh breadcrumbs take an old-fashioned white loaf that's a day or two old, cut off the crusts, cut it into cubes and blitz it in batches in a blender or food processor until you have fine crumbs. (You can freeze any breadcrumbs you don't use straightaway.) Mix the breadcrumbs with the Parmesan, season with pepper and put in a shallow dish.

Beat the egg with the milk in another dish. Put the flour in a third dish and season with salt and pepper. Dip each chicken fillet in the flour, then in the egg mixture then in the breadcrumbs and Parmesan pressing the crumbs in well. Heat the olive oil in a large roasting dish and add the butter. When the foaming dies down turn off the heat and lay the crumbed chicken breasts in the pan. Tilt the pan and spoon the butter and oil mixture over the chicken then put the dish in the oven and cook for 15 minutes. Remove the dish and add the tomatoes, spoon over the juices again. Return to the oven for another 15 minutes, baste once more then cook for a further 10–15 minutes until the chicken pieces are crisp and brown.

YOU COULD ALSO SERVE THE CHICKEN WITH PEAS OR ROAST FENNEL, COOKED AT THE SAME TIME AS THE CHICKEN.

BAKED PORK STEAKS WITH PORTABELLA MUSHROOMS AND MOLTEN CHEESE

This tastes rather like a posh cheeseburger, but looks good enough to serve at a dinner party. You need to use a full-flavoured cheese that melts well like Celtic Promise, Adrahan from Ireland, Reblochon from France or Italian Taleggio.

SERVES 4

Juice of 1 lemon (about 3 tbsp)
4 tbsp olive oil
1 large clove of garlic, peeled and crushed
$1/2$ tsp mild chilli powder or sweet Spanish pimenton
4 lean pork steaks, about 175g each
Salt and pepper
2 large portabella mushrooms, wiped clean and cut into thick slices
110g Celtic Promise or other strong semi-soft cheese, rinded and thinly sliced

Pour the lemon juice and 3 tbsp of the olive oil in a large shallow dish, whisk together with a fork then mix in the crushed garlic, chilli powder and a little salt. Turn the pork steaks in the dish so they are thoroughly coated with the marinade then cover the dish with clingfilm and leave them to marinate for a couple of hours, turning them halfway through. When you're ready to cook the chops pre-heat the oven to 220C/425F/Gas 7. Heat a non-stick frying pan and add a tablespoon of oil. Remove the chops from the marinade, shaking off the excess liquid and brown them for a couple of minutes on each side. Lay them in a baking dish and transfer them to the oven for 12–15 minutes, turning them halfway through. Dip the mushroom slices in the marinade and stir-fry them for a minute or two. When you turn the chops pile the mushrooms on top and lay over the slices of cheese. Cook until brown and bubbling.

GOOD WITH A DARK LEAFY GREEN SALAD AND SOME NEW POTATOES OR TRY SOME **ROAST BUTTERNUT SQUASH** (p147).

HILL LAMB HOTPOT

Lancashire hotpot is one of the great glories of English cooking – the lamb, potatoes and onions all melting into a heavenly goo with the long slow cooking. It's even better made with hill or rare breed lamb.

SERVES 4–6

6 lamb shoulder chops (about 750–800g)
2 level tbsp plain flour
3 tbsp vegetable or light olive oil
40g butter
3 medium to large onions, peeled and thinly sliced (about 450g)
1 large carrot (about 125g), peeled and thinly sliced
1 medium turnip (about 110g) peeled and thinly sliced
750g waxy red potatoes (e.g. Desirée)
125ml dry white wine (e.g. basic French vin blanc, muscadet, pinot grigio)
300ml homemade or fresh shop-bought chicken stock
2 bay leaves
Salt and ground white pepper

You will need a large round or oval lidded casserole.

Trim any excess fat off the chops and pat them dry with kitchen paper. Put the flour into a bowl and season with salt and pepper. Dip the chops into the flour, lightly coating both sides. Heat a large frying pan and add 2 tablespoons of the oil and 15g of the butter. Once the butter has melted, brown the chops on both sides (about 2 minutes a side) and set aside. Add the sliced onions to the oil and butter mixture and fry gently for about 5 minutes, stirring. Add the sliced carrot and turnip and any remaining flour, stir well and set aside. Peel and finely slice the potatoes.

Heat the oven to 200C/400F/Gas 6. Pour the remaining oil in the casserole and wipe it round the base and sides. Put a good layer of sliced potato in the base of the casserole then a layer of vegetables, seasoning each layer lightly with salt and pepper. Arrange the chops on top and tuck in the bay leaves. Tip over the rest of the vegetables spreading them out evenly then arrange the rest of the potato slices neatly on top. Heat the wine and stock in the frying pan and pour carefully over the hotpot. Season lightly with salt and pepper. Melt the remaining butter in the frying pan and pour it over the potato slices. Cover the casserole and place in the oven for about 25 minutes until bubbling gently. Turn the heat down to 150C/300F/Gas 2 and cook for a further two hours, spooning the juices over the potatoes halfway through. Turn up the heat to 200C/400F/Gas 6, remove the lid of the casserole and return to the oven for 30–40 minutes until the potatoes are well browned.

SERVE WITH BRUSSEL TOPS OR SPRING GREENS.

QUICK SAUSAGE, POTATO AND ONION BAKE

A favourite, easy and un-taxing midweek supper dish. Slightly spicy sausages or herby sausages like lamb and mint work well in this recipe.

SERVES 2

450g new or waxy potatoes (like Desirée)
2 medium onions
3–4 cloves of garlic
3 tbsp olive oil

6 plump sausages, with a high meat content (about 400g in total)
Salt and freshly ground black pepper

Preheat the oven to 200C/400F/Gas 6. Scrub the potatoes clean but don't peel them. Cut them into chunky slices (about 4–5cm thick). Peel and thickly slice the onions and garlic. Put all the vegetables in a medium-sized roasting tin with 3 tablespoons of olive oil, season with salt and pepper and mix together well. Roast for 20 minutes, turn the potatoes and onions then lay the sausages on top, turning them so they get a light coating of oil. Cook for another 15 minutes, turn the sausages over then cook for a final 15–20 minutes until the sausages and potatoes are well browned. I don't think this is a dish that needs gravy but if you're a gravy addict feel free (see p34).

SERVE WITH PEAS OR THE **SIMPLE LETTUCE SALAD** (p150).

TOAD-IN-THE-HOLE

No apologies for repeating this sausage classic from my book Sausage & Mash *(Absolute Press, 2004). I can't resist the combination of porky sausages and puffy batter.*

SERVES 4

110g plain flour
$^1/_2$ level tsp salt
2 medium eggs, lightly beaten
175ml semi-skimmed milk mixed with 125ml water
8 herby pork sausages, e.g. Lincolnshire (about 450g–500g)
4 tbsp of grapeseed or rapeseed oil or 1 tbsp oil and 25g of lard or vegetable shortening, diced

You will need a deep rectangular roasting tin about 22 x 28cm.

Sift the flour into a large bowl and sprinkle over the salt. Make a hollow in the centre and add the egg and about a quarter of the milk and water mix. Work the flour into the egg with a wooden spoon until it is all incorporated, beating it briskly until smooth. Gradually add the rest of the milk, beating well between each addition. (Or, easier still, simply bung all the ingredients in the bowl of a food processor and whizz until smooth.) Pour the batter into a jug and leave in the fridge for at least 30 minutes. When the batter is rested heat the oven to 225C/425F/Gas 7. Pour 3 tablespoons of the oil or the diced fat in a large roasting tin and heat till the oil is smoking hot (about 10 minutes).

Meanwhile heat a frying pan, add the remaining oil and brown the sausages lightly on all sides. Take the roasting tin out of the oven, give the batter a final stir or whisk, then pour it into the tin (it should immediately start to bubble up and sizzle). Drop in the sausages one by one with a pair of tongs. Put the pan back in the oven and cook for about 35–40 minutes until the toad is well browned and puffed up. Serve with one of the gravies on p34.

HOT BUTTERED CABBAGE (p132) OR OTHER GREENS ARE GOOD WITH THIS.

BAKED BROWN COW FAGGOTS WITH NEWCASTLE BROWN GRAVY

When I was at university many years ago our landlady used to serve faggots once a week for supper (with chips and peas, of course). I can't say I was anxious to repeat the experience, that is until recently when I spotted them at a farmer's market stall run by the excellent Brown Cow Organics and partnered them with this splendidly robust gravy made from a handy bottle of 'Newky Broon'.

SERVES 4

1 tbsp sunflower oil or vegetable oil
4 large or 8 smaller faggots (about 600g in total)

FOR THE GRAVY

2 tbsp sunflower oil or vegetable oil
1 medium to large onion (about 175g)
1 tsp sugar
1$\frac{1}{2}$ tbsp plain flour
250ml beef stock or stock made with 250ml boiling water and 1 level tsp Bovril
175ml Newcastle Brown ale
1 level tbsp tomato ketchup
Salt, pepper, malt or wine vinegar and Worcestershire sauce to taste.

Preheat the oven to 200F/400F/Gas 6. Put a tablespoon of oil in a baking dish big enough to hold the faggots in a single layer. Turn them in the oil and put them on to bake for 25 minutes, turning them halfway through (If you are using smaller faggots reduce this initial baking time to 15 minutes.)

Meanwhile, make the gravy. Heat the oil in a saucepan over a moderate heat, tip in the onions and mix well, fry over a moderate heat for 5–6 minutes until beginning to brown. Stir in the sugar, cook for a few seconds then add the flour and cook for a few seconds more. Stir in the beef stock, Newcastle Brown and tomato ketchup, bring to the boil then turn down the heat and simmer for 10 minutes. Season to taste with salt, pepper, a few drops of malt or wine vinegar and a few drops of Worcestershire sauce. Take the faggots out of the oven, pour away any excess fat and pour over the gravy. Turn the heat down to 190C/375F/Gas 5, cover the pan and return to the oven for another 10 minutes.

SERVE WITH PEAS AND **SWEET POTATO WEDGES** (p119) THAT YOU CAN BAKE AT THE SAME TIME AS THE FAGGOTS.

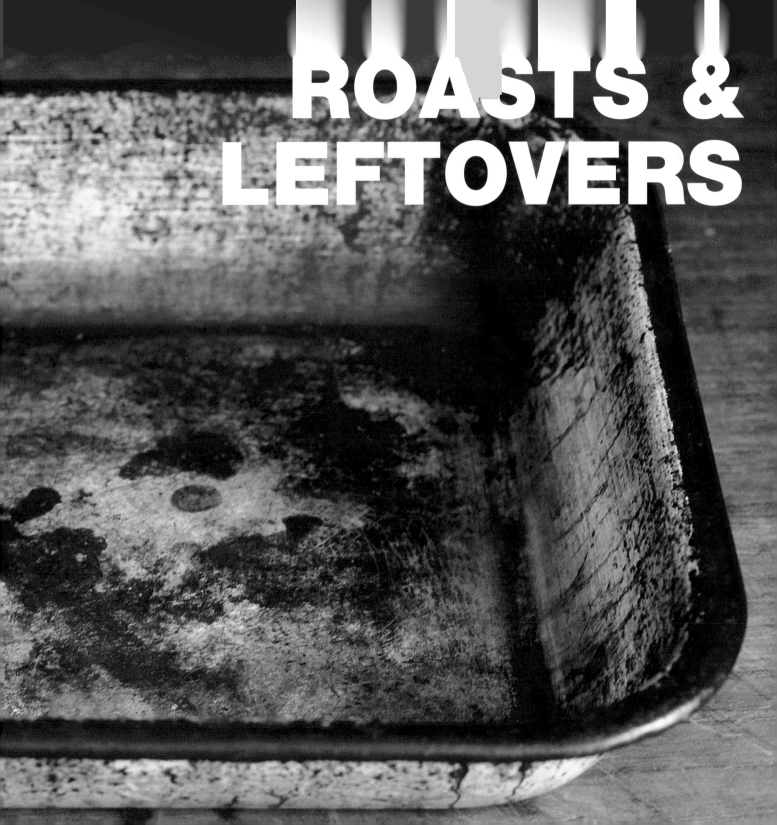

ROASTS & LEFTOVERS

GETTING A GOOD RESULT WITH YOUR ROAST

A roast is one of the simplest things you can cook but it still unnerves many people. What's tricky about it is not the roasting itself, but calculating how long it should take, and how to ensure that the vegetables and other accompaniments are finished at the same time when they may need to share the oven and be cooked at different cooking temperatures.

Most of the latter problems are overcome by letting the meat 'rest' at the end of the cooking period (see below) which has the added bonus of improving the tenderness and texture of the meat. In the meantime you can get on with crisping up the potatoes and making the gravy.

How long you should cook your meat is another issue and one about which a convention has grown up, fuelled by restaurants who cook to order, that most meat should be served rare or just-done. Few would disagree that this suits a steak or a splendid rib of beef but I for one am fed up with

being served half-bloodied birds such as pigeon or duck or inedibly tough lamb, simply because the economics of the modern kitchen dictates that everything must be cooked between the time the order goes in and the time they serve the main course. Don't be ground down by the prevailing rare meat fascism! Try the longer cooking times of Well Done Lamb (p96) or Slow Roast Chicken with Pork and Apple Meatballs (p104) and see if they are to your taste. There are also many splendid roasts such as Slow Roast Belly of Pork (p102) and Pot Roast of Brisket (p95) that benefit from a considerably longer cooking time.

SOME TIPS, MOSTLY OBVIOUS

- Make a note of the weight of the meat when you buy it so you can calculate the cooking time. Some large joints weigh more than domestic scales will register.

- Take the meat out of the fridge for at least 30 minutes before you cook it (longer for a large joint) otherwise

it will mess up your timings.

- Use a (sturdy) roasting tin only slightly bigger than your joint of meat so your precious meat juices don't burn. Unless you're tucking in vegetables alongside, obviously.

- Be conscious that ovens vary in temperature so know your own and make appropriate adjustments to the suggested cooking time. If you don't feel confident about this it might even be worth investing in an oven thermometer (see below).

- Get rid of excess fat as you go. You need a little to baste the meat occasionally but you don't want it swimming in fat. (Chickens, ducks and fattier joints like belly pork produce a lot.) Once you've got rid of most of it (about halfway through the total cooking time) you can replace it with a little stock or other cooking liquid to stop the pan juices burning.

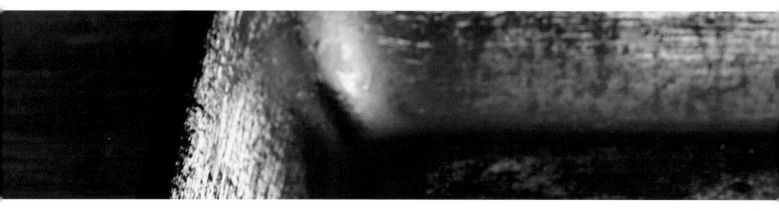

HOW LONG? HOW HOT?

Most roasts benefit from an initial blast of heat to get them going, and all benefit from a final resting period of at least 15 minutes to allow the meat fibres to relax and distribute the heat evenly within the joint. In between, it can cook at a moderate temperature. As a general rule I start a roast at 220C/425F/Gas 7 for 20 minutes, continue at 190C/375F/Gas 5 for 15–20 minutes per 500g, depending how rare I want it, then let it rest for 20 minutes.

It's hard to make hard and fast rules because individual joints vary so much, not merely from one type of meat to another but depending on how they're prepared. A rack of lamb is obviously going to cook at a higher temperature and take a great deal less time than a leg. A rolled piece of meat will take longer than meat on the bone, particularly if it is stuffed and free-range organic meat will take longer than intensively reared meat – not that you're going to buy that, of course....

You can buy a meat thermometer as suggested above, but unless you're a totally inexperienced cook there's a lot to be said for the human eye and the nose. You can smell when a roast has got going. You can see, if you insert a fine skewer into the leg of a chicken, whether the juices are still pink-tinged or running clear. Trust your instinct and experience.

A WORD ON THE IMPORTANT SUBJECT OF GRAVY

For most Brits a roast wouldn't be a roast without gravy, but there aren't many roasts which generate the fabulous meat juices to make their own (the exceptions being beef and turkey) without the addition of some kind of stock, or other flavoursome liquid. Obviously the longer a joint cooks, the more likely you are to get some lovely, sticky caramelised juices to work on.

Nowadays you can buy good fresh stock – at a price – but I find the old solutions of Bovril and Marmite (1 level tsp to 250ml of liquid) work perfectly well and are far better and less synthetic tasting than any ready-made gravy product I've tried. I use Bovril if I want a dark meaty stock or Marmite (or a spoonful of Marigold vegetable bouillon powder) if I want a lighter one. If I want to dilute a gravy which is too thick, I add a spoonful or two of the water I've used to cook the potatoes.

Flour is fundamental to the traditional British gravy – stirred into the meat juices before liquid is added (having poured most of the fat off first). Though with some recipes I prefer to do without flour or add it later, either reducing the cooking liquid by bubbling it furiously, or by whisking in a spoonful or two of butter paste, formed by mashing flour with soft butter (see p58). If you have no meat juices to work on and need a simple gravy you'll find recipes on p34, p36, p68 and p86. In fact there are an amazing array of gravy recipes in this book!

ROAST RIB OF BEEF WITH YORKSHIRE PUDDING

I'm all for being adventurous about food but there are a handful of things with which you don't want to mess. A good joint of beef is one of them. Even the gravy I think should be made the old fashioned way so you have lashings for everyone.

SERVES 6–8

2.5–3kg rib of beef on the bone
2 tbsp light olive oil
Salt and freshly ground black pepper
Mini Yorkshire Puds (see p94)
Horseradish Sauce (see p94)

FOR THE GRAVY

25g plain flour
2 x 284ml tubs fresh beef stock
1 tsp Worcestershire sauce, soy
  sauce or 1/2 tsp Bovril or Marmite
Mushroom ketchup or tomato
  ketchup to taste

Take the beef out of the fridge and allow a couple of hours for it to come to room temperature before cooking it. Preheat the oven to 230C/450F/Gas 8. Smear the meat with 2 tablespoons of olive oil and season well with salt and freshly ground black pepper. Place in a roasting tin and cook for 20 minutes, then reduce the temperature to 190C/375F/Gas 5 and cook for a further 12–14 minutes per 500g, depending how rare you like your beef. Every so often baste with the fat in the tin. Put the potatoes into the oven about half an hour before the beef is due to be ready. When the beef is cooked take it out of the oven and put it on a carving dish. Cover it lightly with foil and leave it in a warm place for at least 20 minutes. Turn up the oven to 220C/425F/Gas 7 to make the Yorkshire pudding and to crisp up the potatoes.

To make the gravy, carefully pour off all except 2–3 tbsp of the fat from the roasting tin (not including the delicious brown sticky bits). Add the flour to the pan and stir thoroughly into the pan juices until they form a thick paste. Cook over a low heat for a few seconds. Take off the heat and add the beef stock bit by bit until you have a smooth thin sauce. Put back over the heat and stir until the gravy thickens. Taste the gravy and see what seasoning it needs. If the meat has made enough tasty juices of its own it may simply be a question of a little salt and pepper and a dash of Worcestershire or soy sauce. If it seems a bit bland add 1/2 a teaspoon of Bovril or Marmite dissolved in a couple of tablespoons of boiling water. Tip in any juices that have run off the beef into the gravy and pour it into a warmed jug.

Once the potatoes and Yorkshire pudding are cooked take the meat to the table and carve. (The easiest way to do this is to cut down the meat by the bone and then cut across the joint in thin slices.) Serve with either horseradish sauce or mustard or both.

CRISPY ROAST POTATOES (p116) ARE OBVIOUSLY A MUST. AND I PERSONALLY LIKE FINE GREEN BEANS WITH ROAST BEEF BUT YOU COULD EQUALLY WELL SERVE CARROTS OR CABBAGE.

continued from p92

MINI YORKSHIRE PUDS

You're more likely to be successful with Yorkshire puddings if you cook them individually instead of in a big tray. A 12–hole deep non-stick muffin tin is perfect.

SERVES 6–8

110g plain flour
$\frac{1}{2}$ level tsp salt
2 medium eggs, lightly beaten
175ml semi-skimmed milk mixed with 125ml water
4 tbsp grapeseed or rapeseed oil

Sift the flour into a large bowl and sprinkle over the salt. Make a hollow in the centre and add the egg and about a quarter of the milk and water mix. Gradually work the flour into the egg with a wooden spoon until it is all incorporated, beating it briskly until smooth. Gradually add the rest of the milk, beating well between each addition. Pour the batter into a jug, cover and leave in the fridge for at least half an hour. Preheat the oven to 220C/425F/Gas 7. Pour a little oil into the bottom of each hole in the muffin pan then heat the pan in the oven till the oil is smoking hot (about 8 minutes). Take the tin out of the oven and pour the batter halfway up the holes in the pan. (It should immediately start to bubble up and sizzle.) Put the pan back in the oven and cook for about 20–25 minutes until the puddings are well browned and puffed up. Serve immediately.

HORSERADISH SAUCE

Horseradish isn't that easy to get hold of so I must confess I generally buy it ready-made. But here's how to do the real thing according to the Constance Spry Cookery Book of 1956.

SERVES 6–8

1 tsp vinegar
A squeeze of lemon juice
$\frac{1}{2}$ tsp English mustard
1–1$\frac{1}{2}$ heaped tbsp freshly grated horseradish
150ml double cream
Salt, pepper and sugar to taste

Mix the vinegar, lemon juice, mustard, seasoning, sugar and horseradish together. Whip the cream until stiff, incorporate the other ingredients and adjust the seasoning. Add extra horseradish if necessary.

STICKY POT-ROAST BRISKET

We're so used to eating beef rare these days that it's easy to forget the virtues of pot-roasting which transforms ordinary cuts like brisket into a sumptuous, sticky treat. This well-used recipe comes from Nicola Cox, a former Sunday Times cook, whose cookery classes I used to go to as an eager-beaver young housewife. Note you have to marinate the meat several hours before you start to cook it – or the day before.

SERVES 4–6

150ml beef stock
150ml red or white wine
1 tbsp wine vinegar
1 clove of garlic, peeled and crushed
1 bay leaf
1 medium onion, peeled and chopped
1 tsp finely chopped fresh thyme
1.35kg boned, rolled brisket of beef
2–3 tbsp dripping or oil
Salt and pepper

Mix the stock and wine with the wine vinegar, garlic, bay leaf, onion and thyme. Put the meat in a bowl, pour over the marinade and rub it in well. Cover the meat and leave in the fridge for 4–24 hours. Preheat the oven to 200C/400F/Gas 6. Remove the meat from the marinade and pat dry with kitchen paper. Strain the marinade. Heat the dripping or oil in a casserole or deep roasting pan, with a lid. Brown the meat all over in the hot fat then add 3–4 tablespoons of the strained marinade. Cover the meat with greaseproof paper, put a lid on the casserole and roast for 2 hours, turning down the temperature to 190C/375F/Gas 5.

Check from time to time that the pan juices are not burning – add more marinade if necessary, but be careful as the flavour of this dish comes from the well-browned sticky juices so do not add too much extra liquid. Once the meat is cooked set it aside in a warm place to rest. Spoon any fat off the surface of the pan juices and add the remaining marinade. Bring to the boil, scraping off all the brown tasty bits from the side of the casserole or tin, and adding a little extra water if necessary. Season to taste with salt and black pepper and serve with the meat.

THIS RECIPE MAKES INTENSELY RICH GRAVY BUT THERE ISN'T MUCH OF IT, SO SERVE IT WITH SOMETHING SLIGHTLY SLOPPY LIKE MASHED POTATO OR A ROOT VEGETABLE MASH LIKE THE **SWEDE AND CARROT MASH** (p128). **BAKED TURNIPS WITH CREAM AND PARMESAN** (p130) WOULD ALSO BE GOOD.

WELL-DONE LAMB WITH
BALSAMIC-GLAZED VEGETABLES

Serving lamb rare, as is common now, is more in the French than the English tradition. Sometimes I think it goes too far. Older lamb in particular is sweeter and more tender if allowed a longer cooking time.

SERVES 4

Half a leg of lamb or mutton (about 1.25kg)
2 tbsp light olive oil or sunflower oil
Salt and freshly ground black pepper
2 medium onions, peeled
2 medium-sized parsnips, peeled
3-4 medium-sized carrots, peeled
1 tbsp balsamic vinegar
225ml lamb stock or light vegetable stock
15g soft butter
15g plain flour

Take the lamb out of the fridge about an hour before you plan to cook it. Preheat the oven to 190C/375F/Gas 5. Put the lamb in a large roasting dish and rub the oil well into it and season with salt and pepper. Roast for an hour. Cut the onions into eight and the carrots and parsnips into four to six pieces. Remove the lamb from the oven, tip any excess fat out of the roasting pan leaving about 2 tablespoons. Add the vegetables and turn in the remaining fat and season with salt and pepper. Return the dish to the oven and cook for 20 minutes. Remove from the oven and turn the vegetables over. Mix the balsamic vinegar with 1 tablespoon of water and drizzle over the meat and vegetables.

Return the pan to the oven for another 20–25 minutes till the vegetables are soft and the lamb cooked. Remove the lamb and vegetables onto a warm carving dish, leaving the juices behind and cover the dish with foil. Rest for at least 10 minutes. Pour the stock into the roasting pan and work any stuck on crusty bits into the gravy. Bring gradually to the boil. Mash the soft butter and flour together on a saucer then add it bit by bit to the gravy, whisking or stirring well. Check the seasoning, adding extra salt and pepper to taste. Add any juices that have accumulated round the roast before carving and serving up.

THERE ARE OBVIOUSLY VEGETABLES INCLUDED WITH THIS BUT YOU MAY ALSO WANT TO SERVE SOME DARK LEAFY GREENS SUCH AS SPRING GREENS OR SAVOY CABBAGE WITH IT. AND SMALL **BAKED POTATOES** (p118) COULD BE COOKED IN THE OVEN AT THE SAME TIME. GIVE THEM ABOUT AN HOUR TO AN HOUR AND A QUARTER.

HERB-CRUSTED RACK OF LAMB WITH ROAST CHERRY TOMATOES

Given the expense of this elegant cut (possibly better known to your butcher as a French-trimmed best end of neck), I would save it for an occasion when you seriously want to impress. How long you cook it obviously depends on how rare you like your meat. I'd give it slightly longer than most chefs suggest, making sure you start it at room temperature.

SERVES 2

1 tbsp olive oil
1 French-trimmed rack of lamb (about 6–7 chops) at room temperature
1 heaped tsp Dijon mustard
8 cherry tomatoes
100ml light vegetable or chicken stock
A few drops of sherry vinegar
Salt and freshly ground black pepper

FOR THE CRUST
30g fresh white breadcrumbs
25g soft butter
1 tsp finely chopped fresh rosemary
1 tbsp finely chopped parsley
1 tbsp finely cut chives
Salt and freshly ground black pepper

Mash together the ingredients for the crust or, easier still, whizz them in a food processor. Preheat the oven to 220C/425F/Gas 7. Heat a small roasting tin or dish on the hob, add a tablespoon of olive oil, then, when it's hot lay the rack of lamb in the dish, fat-side downwards. Cook over a moderate heat for about 3 minutes until nicely browned then, up ending the rack with some kitchen tongs, briefly brown both ends of the meat. Take the dish off the heat, transfer the rack of lamb to a chopping board and pat it dry with kitchen paper. Spread the mustard over the fat side then press and pat in the crumb topping. Wrap the tips of the bones with foil.

Carefully transfer the joint back to the roasting dish, add the cherry tomatoes, turn them in the oil then place in the oven and roast from between 10 minutes (rare) to 20 minutes (medium rare), covering the crust lightly with foil or a butter paper if it starts browning too fast. Take the lamb rack and tomatoes out of the tin, transfer to a warm plate and pour off the fat that has accumulated. Add two thirds of the stock and a few drops of sherry vinegar and work it around the roasting tin, scraping off the caramelised meat juices on the sides. Bubble up and simmer for a few minutes, adding extra stock as needed. (You only need a couple of spoonfuls of pan juices for each helping.) Season to taste with salt and freshly ground black pepper. Pour any accumulated pan juices into the pan, carve the meat into individual chops and serve with the pan juices spooned over.

A **GRATIN DAUPHINOISE** (p120) OR **BAKED TURNIPS WITH CREAM AND PARMESAN** (p130) WOULD BOTH BE GREAT WITH THIS. COOK THEM BEFORE YOU COOK THE LAMB AND SET THEM ASIDE IN A WARM PLACE.

STUFFED LOIN OF LAMB WITH APRICOT, MINT AND PINENUTS

It's very easy to run up a stuffing that helps give a joint a dash of dinner-party glamour. This is an adaptation of a Hugh Fearnley-Whittingstall recipe, adding mint which I always think is irresistible with lamb. You'll need to order this cut from your butcher. Get them to give you the bones; they will enrich the pan juices.

SERVES 4

A 900g–1000g boned loin of lamb
1 tbsp olive oil
150ml dry white wine
Butter paste (made from 1 tsp each
   flour and soft butter – see p58)
Salt and freshly ground black pepper
String for tying the meat

FOR THE STUFFING
20g butter
1 small onion, peeled and very finely
   chopped
1 stick of celery, trimmed and very
   finely sliced
4–5 dried, ready-to-eat apricots, cut
   into small pieces
30g finely chopped pinenuts
40g fresh breadcrumbs from a
   traditional white or wholemeal loaf
2 tbsp finely chopped fresh mint
Salt and pepper

First make the stuffing. Heat a small frying pan over a moderate heat and add the butter. Add the onion and stir and cook for a couple of minutes then add the celery, stir and cook until both vegetables are soft. Off the heat, stir in the apricots, chopped pinenuts and breadcrumbs then stir in the mint and season well. Set aside to cool.

Preheat the oven to 220C/425F/Gas 7. While the oven is heating, open up the meat and lay it out on a flat surface. Pile the stuffing in the middle, cutting a flap in the flesh if you can't quite fit it all in. Roll up the loin and tie at intervals, poking the stuffing back into the meat if it threatens to escape. Put a tablespoon of oil in a small roasting dish or tin and turn the lamb in it. Add any lamb bones if you have some. Season the fat well with salt and pepper. Roast for 20 minutes then turn down the heat to 160C/325F/Gas 3 and roast for a further 20–40 minutes depending how pink you like your lamb. Transfer the meat to a carving dish and cover loosely with foil. Pour the fat off the roasting tin, pour in the white wine and work the crusty bits off the sides of the tin. Bubble up then strain the sauce through a fine sieve. Return to the pan and whisk in the butter paste. Pour in any juices that have accumulated under the meat and season with pepper and salt, if needed. Carve the meat and spoon over the pan juices.

ALMOST ANY GREEN VEGETABLE WILL GO WITH THIS, PARTICULARLY LIGHTLY COOKED BEANS OR BROCCOLI, OR MAKE THE **BRAISED CELERY WITH FENNEL** (p123). A FEW NEW POTATOES WOULD BE NICE TOO.

ROAST LOIN OF PORK WITH PERFECT CRACKLING

Everyone seems to have a different view as to how to get perfect crackling. You rub it with salt. You don't allow salt near it. You rub oil into it. No oil. You pour boiling water over it – once, twice, three times. You baste it... or not. I simply follow the advice of my local butcher, Barry. No salt or oil. Put it in a really hot oven for 25–30 minutes until the crackling starts to form, turn the heat down until the pork is cooked then give it another good blast of heat at the end. What makes the difference of course is having really good pork with a nice dry rind, and keeping the oven as dry and moisture-free as possible i.e. not too many other dishes cooking at the same time. You should also start with the meat at room temperature.

SERVES 6

A large piece of loin of pork (about 2.5kg – six 'chops' in total) with the rind well-scored
1 tbsp of oil
125ml dry white wine
125ml light chicken or vegetable stock
Salt and freshly ground black pepper

You will need a roasting tin with a rack.

Preheat the oven to 230C/450F/Gas 9. Rub a little oil into the lean surfaces of the meat and season with salt and pepper. Put the pork, crackling side up on the rack in the roasting tin then roast for about 20–25 minutes until the crackling starts to sizzle. Turn the heat down to 180C/350F/Gas 4 and cook for 20 minutes per 500g. Halfway through carefully tip away the fat that has accumulated in the pan. When the pork is cooked remove the pork to another roasting dish or tin. (The reason you use another tin is to stop your precious stuck-on juices getting burnt. Otherwise, no gravy!)

Turn the oven back up to 230 C and give the joint another 15 minutes until the crackling is really crisp. Pour away all but a couple of teaspoons of the fat in the first roasting tin and pour in the wine or cider. Work it round the base and edges of the dish, detaching all the stuck-on caramelised juices, then bring to the boil and simmer for a couple of minutes. Add the stock and heat through. Check the seasoning, adding salt and pepper to taste. Turn the heat right down and leave the gravy until you're ready to carve. When the crackling is crisp remove the pork from the oven and set aside on a warm carving plate. Leave it to rest for 10 minutes then carve into thick chops and spoon the gravy over. Serve with apple and onion sauce.

APPLE AND ONION SAUCE

Cook a finely chopped medium onion in a couple of tablespoons of oil until soft. Add 2 large, peeled chopped Bramley apples and a couple of tablespoons of cider or water, put a lid on the pan and cook until the apples are soft and fluffy. Beat with a wooden spoon then season with salt, pepper and a pinch of sugar if you think it needs it.

CRISPY ROAST POTATOES (p116) OF COURSE ARE GREAT WITH THIS. PAR-BOIL THEM THEN PUT THEM IN A ROASTING TIN WITHOUT TOO MUCH OIL SO THAT THEY DON'T STOP THE CRACKLING GETTING CRISP. ANYTHING CABBAGEY IS GOOD TOO – CABBAGE, SPROUTS, DARK LEAFY GREENS....

SLOW-ROAST PORK BELLY WITH PERRY AND FRESH PEAR CHUTNEY

Belly of pork responds really well to long, slow cooking, producing wonderfully tender meat that falls off the bone. I've adapted this recipe from West Country chef Martin Blunos, using perry (pear cider) instead of the original cider.

SERVES 4–6

A large piece of pork belly on the bone (about 1.75–2kg), with the crackling well scored
1 tsp black peppercorns
2 bay leaves
2 cloves of garlic, peeled
750ml dry or medium dry perry (Waitrose does a good one)
250ml chicken stock (optional)
2 tsp butter paste (see p58)
Salt, pepper and lemon juice or cider vinegar to taste

You will need a large, lidded roasting tin, or an open tin and some baking parchment and foil.

Preheat the oven to 150C/300F/Gas 2. Put the peppercorns and bay leaves in a large roasting tin. Place the pork on top, skin side upwards, add the peeled garlic and pour in 500ml of the perry and 750ml water. Cover with a tight fitting lid or a sheet of baking parchment and a large sheet of foil, well tucked round the edges. Cook for about 3 hours, turning the heat down a touch after 45 minutes once you smell the meat cooking (don't be tempted to open it up and peek). Once the meat is cooked, pour off the juices into a large bowl and leave to cool for about 10 minutes (leave a little juice behind in the roasting tin). Increase the heat in the oven to 200C/400F/Gas 6. Return the pork to the oven and cook for another 15–20 minutes until the crackling has browned then remove to a carving plate and keep warm. (If you want crisper crackling cut away the skin in a single piece and put it on a baking sheet. Turn up the oven to 225C/425F/Gas 7 – covering or removing any vegetables that might be cooking there – and cook the crackling for a further 10 minutes until crisp.)

Skim the fat off the reserved cooking juices. Pour off the remaining fat from the roasting tin and place it on a gas burner or electric ring. Pour in the remaining perry and bubble up until it has reduced by a third, then add 250ml of the skimmed cooking liquid (or 250ml chicken stock if you find the cooking liquid too fatty). Bring to the boil then reduce the heat and simmer for 10 minutes. Whisk in a little butter paste to thicken then season with salt, pepper and a squeeze of lemon juice or a few drops of cider vinegar. Carve the meat into rough chunks and serve with the pan juices and the Fresh Pear Chutney.

FRESH PEAR 'CHUTNEY'

2 tbsp sunflower oil
15g butter
3–4 conference pears, peeled and cut into small chunks
2 tbsp unrefined caster sugar
2 tbsp cider vinegar
4–5 tbsp of the pork braising liquid (above) or chicken stock
2 cloves
Salt and pepper

Heat the oil in a saucepan, add the butter and once it has melted add the chopped pears. Stir and cook for 3–4 minutes over a moderate heat. Add the sugar and cook for a few more minutes until the pear starts to brown then pour in the cider vinegar and bubble up. Add 4–5 tablespoons of the pork braising liquid or chicken stock and the cloves and simmer until the pears are tender. Season with salt and pepper and extra cider vinegar if you think it needs sharpening up.

THIS GOES WELL WITH SOME BOILED (PREFERABLY NEW) POTATOES IN THEIR SKINS AND A LARGE TRAY OF **ROAST ROOT VEG WITH FENNEL AND CORIANDER** (p124). YOU COULD ALSO SERVE IT WITH **HOT BUTTERED CABBAGE** (p132).

SUGAR-GLAZED GAMMON WITH CIDER

Roast gammon seems to be curiously unfashionable but I love the sweet-sour flavour of the salty ham and the crunchy sugary crust. I also like to make it the traditional way by soaking and boiling it first rather than roasting it. It takes a little longer but it's much less salty and you end up with a sweeter, more succulent joint. Try to find a piece of gammon that has a good expanse of skin to glaze. I've given the recipe for a small joint but you can just as easily make it for larger numbers by doubling the quantities.

SERVES 3–4

A 750g joint of smoked gammon
500ml dry cider
2 tbsp Demerara sugar
$\frac{1}{2}$ tsp dry English mustard
6 cloves

Soak the gammon for several hours or overnight. Place in a pan with the cider and enough fresh water to cover, bring slowly to the boil, part cover the pan and simmer gently for 45 minutes. When the cooking time is nearly up preheat the oven to 220C/425F/Gas 7. Remove the meat and set aside to cool for a few minutes. Cut off the rind and score the fat in a diamond pattern. Mix together the sugar and mustard and pat it into the fat, inserting the cloves where the lines cross. Place in a roasting tin with a few spoonfuls of the cooking liquid. Cover the lean part of the meat with foil, transfer to the oven and roast for about 15 minutes, or until the crust is nicely browned. Set aside to rest for 10–15 minutes before carving.

AS THERE ARE NO ROASTING JUICES IT'S BEST TO SERVE THIS WITH A VEGETABLE DISH WITH A SAUCE LIKE **CAULIFLOWER CHEESE** (p136) OR **CREAMED LEEKS** (p119) OR A GRATIN SUCH AS THE **GRATIN OF BRUSSEL SPROUTS** (p130).

SLOW ROAST CHICKEN WITH PORK AND APPLE MEATBALLS AND CREAMY CIDER SAUCE

The longer-than-usual cooking time and the liquid in the roasting tin result in a very tender, tasty bird.

SERVES 4–5

A medium-to-large-sized organic
  chicken (about 1.8kg)
4 tbsp olive or sunflower oil
1 medium-sized onion
1 medium-sized dessert apple
  (e.g. Cox or Blenheim)
350ml good quality dry cider
2 tbsp crème fraîche
Sea salt and black pepper

FOR THE PORK AND APPLE MEATBALLS

350g traditional plain pork sausages
  with a high meat content
1 small onion, peeled and finely
  chopped
1 medium sized dessert apple (Cox or
  Blenheim), peeled and finely chopped
50g fresh white breadcrumbs
2 tbsp finely chopped fresh parsley
1 medium egg
2 tbsp plain flour

First make the meatballs. Skin the sausages and break up the sausage meat in a bowl. Add the onion, apple, fresh breadcrumbs and parsley and mix together thoroughly. Add half the beaten egg and mix again. You should have a mixture that sticks together but which is not too wet. Add extra egg if necessary. Leave for ten minutes, then with floured hands, form the mixture into balls approximately the size of a large walnut. Roll in flour and set aside (you can do this bit of the preparation in advance).

Smear the chicken with half the olive oil, season with salt and pepper and place in a large roasting tin in a pre-heated oven at 200C/400F/Gas 6. Cook for 30 minutes then pour off any fat. Peel and cut the remaining apple and onion into thick slices and arrange them round the meat. Pour over the cider. Turn the oven down to 190C/375F/Gas 5 and cook for a further

15 minutes. Heat the remaining olive oil in a frying pan and fry the meatballs on all sides until they are nicely browned. Add to the roasting tin, spooning over the pan juices. Return to the oven for another 30–45 minutes until the meatballs and chicken are cooked, covering the chicken breast with foil if it's getting too brown. (Insert a skewer or sharp knife in the thickest part of the chicken leg to check it's done; the juices should run clear.) Remove the chicken and meatballs from the pan and keep in a warm place. Mash the onions and apples in the remaining liquid in the tin then strain into a bowl. Return the strained sauce to the roasting tin and heat through, allowing it to bubble up for a few minutes to thicken and reduce. Take off the heat and leave for a couple of minutes, then stir in the crème fraîche. Check the seasoning, adding extra salt and pepper as necessary and serve separately.

WITH ALL THE LIQUID IN THE ROASTING TIN, ROAST POTATOES ARE NOT GOING TO BROWN TOO WELL SO I SUGGEST YOU SERVE **PAN-ROAST POTATOES** (p116) INSTEAD, TOGETHER WITH A SIMPLY COOKED GREEN VEGETABLE SUCH AS RUNNER BEANS OR SPROUTS.

ROAST GUINEAFOWL WITH BREAD SAUCE, BACON AND HOT KETTLE CHIPS

Guineafowl makes a good, quick roast for two, especially with these easy accompaniments. (Kettle chips make a great substitute for game chips.) Start the bread sauce before you put on the roast to leave plenty of time for the onion and other flavours to infuse.

SERVES 2

1 tbsp olive oil
1 small guineafowl
6 thinly sliced streaky bacon rashers
100 ml chicken stock or a mixture of white wine and stock
Salt and freshly ground pepper
A small pack (or two) of Kettle chips or other premium potato crisps

Preheat the oven to 220C/425F/Gas 7. Smear the guineafowl with olive oil, season with salt and pepper and place, breast side upwards in a small roasting tin or cast-iron enamel dish.

Roast for 30 minutes, pour off the fat, lay the bacon pieces over the breast and cook for another 20–25 minutes until the bird and the bacon are well browned. Take the guineafowl out of the oven and leave to rest in a warm place for 10–15 minutes. Pour away any fat in the roasting dish, add the stock, work it around the sides of the dish to pick up all the caramelised cooking juices and reduce until you have 3–4 spoonfuls of liquid. Season to taste with salt and pepper. Just before serving place the Kettle chips on a tray and heat for 2 minutes in the oven. Carve the guineafowl and serve with the crisps, bacon, bread sauce and pan juices.

BREAD SAUCE

4 cloves
1 medium onion, peeled and halved
1 large clove of garlic, peeled (optional but good)
1 bay leaf
300ml full cream milk
75g fresh breadcrumbs
Salt, freshly ground pepper and a little freshly grated nutmeg
15g butter
1 tbsp finely chopped parsley (optional)

Stick the cloves in both halves of the onion, place in a small saucepan with the garlic and bay leaf, pour over the milk and heat until just below boiling point. Turn the heat down to a bare simmer and cook for 15 minutes then set the milk aside for another 15 minutes so that the flavours can continue infusing. Put the breadcrumbs in a bowl and strain over the warm milk, then tip the sauce back into the saucepan and heat gently over a low heat for about 10 minutes until thick. Season with salt, pepper and a little freshly grated nutmeg. Just before serving add the butter and finely chopped parsley, if using.

SOME HOT BUTTERED CABBAGE (p132) OR STIR-FRIED SPROUTS WITH CASHEW NUTS (p132) WOULD GO WELL.

SUMMER ROAST POUSSIN WITH LOOSE LEMON AND PARSLEY STUFFING

The ideal roast for hot weather. Leaving the stuffing loose retains its lightness and freshness.

SERVES 2–4

2 x 450g poussins
1 tbsp olive oil
15g butter
100ml light chicken or vegetable
  stock or stock made with 1 tsp
  vegetable bouillon powder
Salt and pepper

FOR THE STUFFING

50g butter
2 tbsp olive oil
100g fresh white breadcrumbs made
  from a traditional loaf
Finely grated rind of 1 unwaxed lemon
4 heaped tbsp finely chopped parsley
Salt and pepper

Preheat the oven to 220C/425F/Gas 7. Heat 1 tbsp of oil together with 15g of butter until the butter melts and brush it over the poussins. Season with salt and pepper. Roast the poussins for 20 minutes then turn the heat down to 190C/375F/Gas 5 and cook for a further 30–40 minutes until the poussins are cooked. Set aside to rest while you make the stuffing and gravy. Heat the oil for the stuffing in a large frying pan. Add the butter and wait until the foaming dies down then tip in the fresh breadcrumbs. Stir for a minute so that the crumbs absorb the butter and oil, then add the lemon rind and parsley and stir for a couple of minutes until beginning to crisp. Season with salt and pepper and keep warm over a low heat. Pour the fat off the dish you used to roast the poussins and pour in the stock. Heat gently, scraping off the stuck-on juices round the side of the pan.

Bubble up and reduce by half. Pour in the juices that have accumulated under the poussins and season with salt and pepper. Split the poussins in two down the backbone and serve with the stuffing and some of the gravy spooned over.

ONE-MINUTE COURGETTES (p147) AND **RUNNER BEAN PUREE** (p140) GO WELL WITH THIS. OR YOU COULD SERVE SOME SIMPLY STEAMED BROCCOLI.

HAIR-DRIED DUCK

Yes, you did read that right! This recipe involves a hair-dryer. I got the idea from Kevin Gould's book Dishy *that suggests it as an alternative to the Chinese way of hanging duck in the open air to get a super-crisp skin. There are, admittedly, simpler ways of cooking duck but children absolutely love it and it's a great way to get them into the kitchen.*

SERVES 4

1 Gressingham duck, about 2kg in
  weight, with its giblets
About 2 litres of hot chicken or
  vegetable stock mixed with 1 tbsp
  Chinese five spice seasoning
Sea salt

FOR THE GIBLET GRAVY
1 onion, peeled and quartered
1 carrot, peeled and chopped
Soy sauce or Marmite to taste

You will need a very large saucepan
  or deep casserole to fit the duck.

Take the duck out of the fridge at least an hour before you plan to cook it. Remove the giblets (keeping the liver to cook later) and any large chunks of fat inside the carcass. Put the duck in the saucepan, breast-side downwards and pour over enough boiling stock to cover it. Partially cover the pan, bring back to the boil then turn the heat down and simmer for 40 minutes, turning the duck halfway through. Remove the duck from the pan, and set aside till cool enough to handle (about 10 minutes). Pat it dry with kitchen paper and place on a rack in a roasting tin, making sure the tin is well away from any water. Plug in the hairdryer (without a diffuser or nozzle) and turn up to the highest setting. Dry the duck all over for about 15 minutes (you should see the fat running off it). Pat dry again with kitchen paper and set the duck aside until ready to cook. (You can cool it completely and refrigerate it at this stage.) Discard the fat from the tin (and save for roasting potatoes).

While the duck is cooking make a stock from the giblets. Set aside the liver then chop the remaining giblets roughly and brown in a little oil. Add the onion and carrot and fry for another 5 minutes until well browned. Add about 600ml water and simmer for half an hour until the stock is reduced by about a third. Strain and keep to use in the gravy (below).

When ready to finish the duck preheat the oven to 200C/400F/Gas 6. Lay the duck breast- side upwards and rub the skin with sea salt, roast for 30–45 minutes. Pour off the fat every 15 minutes or so. When completely cooked (any juices that run out when you pierce the skin should be completely clear) set aside and keep warm.

Pour off any excess fat from the pan, pour in about 300ml of giblet stock and work it round the pan, loosening the sticky residues. Bubble up and boil fiercely for 5 minutes until reduced. Season to taste (you may want to add a little soy sauce or $^1/_2$ teaspoon of Marmite dissolved in 2 tablespoons of hot water) and strain into a warm jug. Slice the duck liver, fry for a few seconds in a little butter and give some to whoever wants it.

FRENCH PEAS (p139) ARE THE IDEAL ACCOMPANIMENT FOR THIS TOGETHER WITH SOME NEW POTATOES. OR SERVE SIMPLY COOKED PEAS AND **GRILLED PARSNIPS WITH HONEY AND ROSEMARY** (p129).

LEFTOVERS

Leftovers have always been a major part of the 'meat and two veg' philosophy – the best bit, many would say. A Sunday roast could be made to stretch for 3 days at least – cold on Monday, turned into a shepherd's or cottage pie on Tuesday, the scraps curried on Wednesday.

I was never too keen on the latter two options. Shepherd's pie or cottage pie are both better made with fresh mince, though a little extra chopped rare leftover beef or lamb can be slipped in to bulk it out without the whole dish taking on that rubbery, shoe leather consistency that cold roast meat can acquire when reheated in gravy or stock.

Fried meat works better (see the Roast Beef Hash on p112) but the best leftovers are undoubtedly cold, served at room temperature rather than fridge cold – indeed better, though the health police will probably get me for saying this, not refrigerated at all but kept in a larder or other cool place. Not indefinitely, obviously, but for up to 24 hours.

Because you have nothing to do to the main ingredient of your meal, apart from slicing it up, you may have time to make an interesting vegetable dish like a gratin to go with it. Here are some ideas paired with dishes from the veg section:

COLD ROAST BEEF

Roast beef hash (p112), Flash-roast potatoes with garlic and mushrooms (p119) Steamed Summer Vegetables with tomatoes, pinenuts and basil (p142), the asparagus and mushroom side dish on p16 and the green sauce opposite.

COLD ROAST LAMB

Gratin Dauphinoise, Jansson's Temptation (p120), Slow Baked Onions with Butter and Rosemary (p122), Spiced Carrot and Spring Onion Fritters (p127), Grilled Parsnips with Honey and Rosemary (p129) Ratatouille (p144) Courgette and Tomato Gratin (p146), Garlicky Green Beans (p140).

COLD ROAST PORK OR HAM

Creamed Leeks (p123), Roast Root Veg with Fennel and Coriander (p124), Gratin of Brussel Sprouts (p130), Cauliflower Cheese (p136) A Good Old-Fashioned English Salad (p148), Russian Salad (p151).

COLD ROAST CHICKEN OR TURKEY

Pan-roast potatoes (p116), Stir fried Sprouts with Cashew Nuts (p132) Warm Broccoli Salad (p138), Runner Bean Purée (p140), Cucumber and Chive salad (p150) and cold Bread Sauce and the Loose Lemon and Parsley Stuffing on p107 (not that they're veg, but they're good!).

COLD ROAST DUCK

Baked Turnips with Cream and Parmesan (p130), Purple Sprouting Broccoli with Blood Orange Butter (p138) Watercress, Orange and Walnut Salad (p151).

GREEN SAUCE (AKA SALSA VERDE)

I much prefer the Italian version of green sauce to the traditional British one where herbs are added to a white sauce or mayonnaise. It's particularly good with leftover rare roast beef.

SERVES 4–6

4 heaped tbsp finely chopped curly parsley
1 heaped tbsp finely chopped mint leaves
2 heaped tbsp finely chopped basil leaves
About 100ml extra virgin olive oil
3 spring onions, trimmed and finely chopped
2 cloves of garlic, peeled and finely chopped
2 tbsp capers, rinsed and finely chopped
1 tbsp rinsed and finely chopped gherkins
5 anchovy fillets, finely chopped
2 tsp Dijon mustard
2 tbsp red wine vinegar
Freshly ground black pepper

Put the chopped herbs in a bowl with most of the oil. Stir and add the spring onions, garlic, capers, gherkins and anchovy fillets. Mix in the Dijon mustard and wine vinegar then add enough olive oil to make it slightly sloppy. Season to taste with freshly ground black pepper. You shouldn't need salt.

CORONATION CHICKEN

Believe it or not Coronation chicken, which was invented to celebrate the Queen's coronation in 1953, is actually quite a complicated recipe. My version is simply an easy way of zipping up leftover chicken or turkey.

SERVES 2

350–400g leftover chicken or turkey meat (breast or thigh rather than drumsticks)
Crisp lettuce leaves
25g toasted flaked almonds or chopped cashew nuts
A few chopped coriander leaves (optional)

FOR THE DRESSING
2 heaped tbsp mayonnaise
2 heaped tbsp plain yoghurt or low-fat crème fraîche
2–3 tbsp mango chutney or 1–2 tsp curry paste and 2–3 tbsp soft-set apricot jam
1–2 tsp of tomato ketchup (optional)
Salt, freshly ground black pepper and lemon juice to taste

To toast the almonds or cashew nuts put them in a small frying pan over a low heat, turning them occasionally until they're lightly browned.

Remove any skin from the chicken and slice thickly. Mix together the mayo, yoghurt and mango chutney or curry paste and apricot jam. Adjust the quantities of any of these to taste, adding a little tomato ketchup to round out the flavour and season with salt, pepper and a squeeze of lemon juice. Pour over the prepared chicken and toss together. Lay a few crisp lettuce leaves on a plate and spoon over the chicken. Sprinkle over the toasted nuts and some roughly chopped coriander leaves if you have some.

A BIT OF CRUNCH IN THE FORM OF SOME SLICED CELERY, DE-SEEDED CUCUMBER OR DICED RED PEPPER SCATTERED ON TOP OF THE LETTUCE WOULD GO DOWN WELL.

ROAST BEEF HASH

A great way to use up the last scraps of a joint, but, like most leftover recipes, this can be adapted depending on what you have available. I've used cooked new potatoes as they hold their shape marginally better than old ones. Not that it matters hugely.

SERVES 2

25g beef dripping or 2 tbsp olive oil
1 medium onion, peeled and roughly chopped or $\frac{1}{2}$ a bunch of spring onions
300g cooked boiled potatoes, diced
250g–300g cold roast beef, ideally rare, cut into cubes
3 tbsp finely chopped parsley
A spoonful or two of jellied meat stock or gravy, if you have some
A few shakes of Worcestershire sauce and/or a few drops of soy sauce
Salt and pepper

Heat a large frying pan and add the beef dripping or oil. Add the onion and fry over a moderate heat for 3–4 minutes until beginning to brown. Tip in the diced potatoes and continue to fry until both the potatoes and onion are browned. Add the beef, stir and fry for another couple of minutes, then stir in the parsley and jellied stock or gravy (not too much – you don't want it soggy). Heat through for a minute then shake over a little Worcestershire sauce and/or soy sauce. Season to taste with salt and freshly ground black pepper and serve with ketchup, brown sauce, chilli sauce or horseradish sauce – whatever you fancy.

YOU COULD SERVE THIS WITH **GARLIC GREENS** (p133), **HOT BUTTERED CABBAGE** (p132) OR A GREEN SALAD.

JUST VEG

CRISPY ROAST POTATOES

To get really crispy roast potatoes you need to par-boil them first.

SERVES 4–6

1.5 kg good quality roasting potatoes such as King Edwards, peeled and halved or quartered depending on size
4 tbsp groundnut or rapeseed oil or 2 tbsp of oil and 25g beef dripping if you're roasting beef

Put the potatoes in a large saucepan, cover them with cold water and bring them to the boil. Skim off any froth and cook the potatoes for 5 minutes. Drain the potatoes in a colander and shake well to rough up the edges. Transfer them to a large roasting tin with the oil, or oil and dripping, and turn them so that they are coated on all sides. Cook for 45 minutes at 200C/400F/Gas 6 (or whatever temperature you're cooking the roast) then turn up the heat to 220C/425F/Gas 7 and cook for a further 15–25 minutes until the potatoes are well browned and crisp.

PAN-ROAST POTATOES

If for any reason you can't use the oven to cook roast potatoes these are a good alternative – halfway between a roast and a sauté potato in texture.

SERVES 4

500g baby new potatoes, washed and dried
1 tbsp olive oil
Maldon sea salt

Take a casserole big enough to hold the potatoes in a single layer. Heat the casserole over a moderate heat, add the oil then tip in the potatoes. Give the pan a good shake and cover. Cook for about 25–40 minutes depending on the size of the potatoes and the thickness of the pan, shaking the pan regularly to ensure the potatoes brown evenly. Add a tablespoon of water now and then, if they seem to be catching. When the potatoes are tender sprinkle over a little Maldon sea salt, rubbed between your fingers.

SAUTE POTATOES

Somehow these don't seem as indulgent as chips though they obviously are....

SERVES 2–3

350g waxy potatoes, e.g. Desirée
150ml groundnut or rapeseed oil
Sea salt

You will need a wok or large deep frying pan, but if you have a deep-fat fryer obviously you can cook them in that.

Peel the potatoes and cut into even-sized cubes. Rinse in cold water and dry with a clean tea towel. Heat the oil in a wok for about 3 minutes or until hot enough to brown a cube of bread in a few seconds. Tip the potato pieces into the wok and fry, moving them around the wok with a long-handled slotted spoon. When they begin to colour remove them from the wok with the slotted spoon, let the oil reheat for a minute or two then return the potatoes to the pan until crisp and brown. Drain on kitchen paper and sprinkle with salt.

BAKED POTATOES

One of my pet moans is why shops sell such enormous baking potatoes. They take an age to cook and make it really hard to get the centre soft and fluffy and the skin nice and crisp. Buy medium-sized ones and have two if you feel short-changed.

SERVES 4–6

4–6 evenly-sized potatoes, about
  250–300g each
A little sunflower or olive oil
30–40g chilled but not over-cold
  butter

Preheat the oven to 200C/400F/Gas 6. Wash the potatoes and dry with kitchen paper. Prick the skin with a fork in several places beforehand to ensure the potatoes don't burst (not necessary if you have a potato spike). Pour a little oil into your palms and rub it over the potatoes. Put the potatoes on a baking tray or in a roasting tin for about an hour, turning them halfway through. Cut a cross in the centre of each baked potato as you take it out of the oven then, protecting your hands with oven gloves, squeeze the sides of the

potato so that it opens up at the top. (This lets the steam escape and makes the potato fluffier.) Insert a knob of butter in each potato. Good with stews and casseroles.

FLASH-ROAST POTATOES WITH GARLIC AND MUSHROOMS

This is the potato dish my friend Richard serves with his legendary barbecues. It can be prepared well ahead then just given a quick blast in a hot oven to finish it. Oddly it makes the button mushrooms taste like ceps.

SERVES 4–6

750g small new potatoes, well scrubbed
4 tbsp olive oil
350g button mushrooms, washed and thickly sliced
3 cloves of garlic, peeled and thinly sliced
3 tbsp roughly chopped flat-leaf parsley
Salt and freshly ground pepper

Cut the potatoes into even-sized pieces, the size of the smallest potatoes. Put them in a saucepan, cover them with boiling water, bring them back to the boil and cook for 5 minutes. Drain the potatoes and tip into a roasting tin. Heat the olive oil in a wok or large frying pan and add the sliced mushrooms. Stir-fry for a minute or two then add the garlic. Fry for a minute then take off the heat and tip the mushrooms over the potatoes. Season well with salt and pepper and mix thoroughly. When you're ready to cook the potatoes preheat the oven to 220C/425F/Gas 8. Roast the potatoes and mushrooms for 15–20 minutes until nicely browned, turning them halfway through. Stir in the fresh parsley and serve. Good with any kind of roast or grill.

SWEET POTATO WEDGES

Sweet potatoes make a good alternative to ordinary potatoes, especially with rich stews or dishes like the Baked Brown Cow Faggots on p86.

SERVES 4

4 medium-sized sweet potatoes
2 tbsp light olive oil or sunflower oil
A hot spice grind mix or a few coriander seeds, crushed chillies and coarse salt roughly crushed together with a pestle and mortar

Preheat the oven to 200C/400F/Gas 6. Scrub the potatoes clean, pat dry then cut into 4 lengthways. Put the wedges in a baking dish, trickle over 2 tablespoons of oil and turn the potatoes in the oil so all sides are coated. Season with the spice mix, or with the other seasonings and bake for about 40 minutes or until soft, turning the potatoes halfway through.

GRATIN DAUPHINOISE

Not very PC in these health-conscious days but undoubtedly one of the world's great potato dishes.

SERVES 6

284 ml carton whipping cream
2 cloves of garlic, peeled and cut into
  thin slices
750g Desirée potatoes
25g butter plus a bit extra for
  buttering the dish
100ml semi-skimmed milk
2 tbsp fresh Parmesan
Salt and freshly ground black pepper

Heat the oven to 190C/375F/Gas 5. Pour the cream into a small saucepan and heat very gently with the sliced garlic. Leave to infuse while you peel the potatoes and cut them into very thin slices. Butter a shallow ovenproof dish and place a layer of potatoes over the bottom. Dot a bit of butter over the potato and season with salt and pepper. Repeat until all the potatoes are used. Pour over the warm cream and enough milk to come almost to the top of the potatoes. Sprinkle with grated Parmesan and bake for an hour to an hour and a quarter until the top is browned and the potatoes cooked through.

JANSSON'S TEMPTATION

I was first introduced to this aptly named potato dish by one of our Swedish au pairs. It's particularly good with cold roast beef or lamb. It's best made with what are labelled Swedish 'anchovies' but are actually sprat fillets pickled in an aromatic brine which gives a special character to the dish. You can buy them in IKEA.

SERVES 6

1kg waxy potatoes such as Desirée
1 large mild Spanish onion (about 250g)
2 x 50g tins of Swedish anchovies or 2 x 50g tins ordinary anchovies in olive oil
300ml full cream milk plus another 150ml for soaking the anchovies if necessary (see method)
284ml carton of double cream
Ground black pepper
15g of chilled butter

Preheat the oven to 200C/400F/Gas 6. If you are not using Swedish anchovies, drain and soak the anchovies in 150ml of milk for at least $^{1}/_{2}$ an hour. Peel the potatoes and cut into thin, matchstick-sized chips. Peel and finely slice the onion. Drain and finely chop the anchovies. Generously butter a large shallow ovenproof dish and layer up the potatoes, onions and anchovies, finishing with a layer of potatoes. Season each layer as you go with black pepper. Mix the cream and the remaining milk and pour carefully over the dish. Dot the top with butter. Cover loosely with lightly greased foil and bake for 45 minutes. Remove the foil and cook for a further 20–30 minutes or until the potatoes are thoroughly cooked and the top of the dish is well browned.

SLOW-BAKED ONIONS WITH BUTTER AND ROSEMARY

Baked onions are one of the classic accompaniments to an English roast, but if you want to get the maximum sweet flavour out of them, it's better to cook them on their own rather than round the meat.

SERVES 6

6 medium-sized onions (about 100g each)

40g soft butter plus another 25g for buttering the foil

2 tsp finely chopped fresh rosemary or thyme leaves

Salt and freshly ground black pepper

Cut the tops off the onions and peel away the papery skin and any damaged outer layers. Put the onions in a saucepan, cover with boiling water, bring back to the boil and simmer for 5 minutes. Drain and leave until cool enough to handle. Mash the soft butter with the rosemary and season with salt and pepper. Cut or tear six squares of foil big enough to enclose an onion and rub generously with soft butter. Cut each of the onions vertically two thirds of the way down and put a little of the rosemary butter in the middle. Lay each onion on a piece of buttered foil and fold over the foil at the top. Heat the oven to 190C/375F/Gas 5 (if you don't already have the oven on for a roast) and bake the onions for about $1^1/_2$–$1^3/_4$ hours, adding a little water to the baking dish if the buttery juices start to escape. Turn the heat up to 220C/425F/Gas 7 and open the foil up. Roast the onions for another 15 minutes until lightly browned. Particularly good with roast lamb or pork.

CREAMED LEEKS

Do buy loose leeks for this with plenty of green on them, rather than pre-wrapped squeaky clean, trimmed leeks; they have so much more flavour.

SERVES 4

3–4 medium-sized leeks
30g butter
1½ tbsp plain flour
300ml semi-skimmed milk
2–3 tbsp double or whipping cream
(optional)
Salt and pepper
1 tbsp finely chopped parsley
(optional)

Cut off the top of the green leaves and remove any damaged or coarse outer leaves. Cut the leeks in half lengthways almost to the roots and rinse thoroughly taking care to wash in between the leaves. Finely slice the leeks then rinse them again. Melt the butter in a non-stick saucepan, add the leeks, stir, cover and cook for 4–5 minutes until soft. Stir in the flour then gradually add the milk, stirring all the time. Bring to the boil then turn the heat down and simmer for 5 minutes until thick. Stir in the cream. Season with salt and pepper. Stir in the parsley, if using and serve. Good with roast or boiled gammon or cold ham.

BRAISED CELERY WITH FENNEL

Celery is a hugely underestimated vegetable, as this recipe, I hope, demonstrates.

SERVES 4

1 head of celery, with leaves if possible, washed, trimmed and sliced
25g butter
1 medium to large onion, peeled and finely chopped
½ tsp fennel seeds
¼ tsp dried thyme
¼ tsp sea salt
¼ tsp black peppercorns
300ml chicken, duck or game stock or 2 tsp vegetable bouillon powder

Put the celery (except for the leaves) in a saucepan, cover with boiling water and bring to the boil. Simmer for 5 minutes, drain, retaining the water if you don't have any stock. Heat the butter in a lidded saucepan or casserole, add the onion and cook over a low heat for about 3–4 minutes until soft. Grind the spices together with a pestle and mortar and add to the onion. Stir, tip in the celery, pour in the stock or bouillon powder and the cooking water to just cover the celery, bring to the boil, cover, turn the heat down and simmer for about 15–20 minutes until the celery is tender. Remove the lid, turn up the heat and cook fast until the liquid has virtually disappeared (another 10–15 minutes) adding the leaves once the liquid has reduced by half. Good with roast pork or a rich dish like oxtail.

ROAST ROOT VEG WITH FENNEL AND CORIANDER

Fennel makes a particularly good addition to a tray of roast root vegetables, particularly if you're serving it with pork or chicken.

SERVES 4–6

2 medium bulbs of fennel (about 300g)
1 large or 2 medium parsnips (about 300g)
3 carrots (about 250g)
2 medium onions (about 200g)
4 tbsp sunflower or light olive oil
1½ tsp coriander seeds, crushed
Salt and pepper

Preheat the oven to 200C/400F/Gas 6. Trim the base and any leaves off the fennel and cut into wedges. Peel the parsnips, cut in half then halve again or quarter depending how thick they are, removing the central woody core. Peel and halve the carrots lengthways then cut in half or quarters. Peel the onions and cut into quarters. Put all the vegetables in a large roasting tin, pour over the oil, sprinkle over the coriander and season generously with salt and pepper. Toss well together and bake for about 45–50 minutes until the vegetables are soft and browned.

SLOW-ROAST CARROTS

A good way of cooking carrots that brings out all their natural sweetness.

SERVES 4

450g carrots, peele
1 tbsp olive oil
Salt and pepper

Preheat the oven to 180C/350F/Gas 4. Cut the carrots into evenly sized diagonal slices and put in a roasting tin. Pour over the oil and season with salt and pepper. Cook for about 40–45 minutes until soft.

BRAISED CARROTS

Like most vegetables, carrots taste much more intense when they're cooked with the minimum amount of water. They also look much sexier cut on the slant instead of in rounds.

SERVES 4

1 tbsp oil
A small slice (about 15g) butter
450g carrots, peeled and cut on the slant
1 tsp vegetable bouillon powder
Salt and freshly ground black pepper
1 tbsp fresh parsley, finely chopped (optional)

Heat a small casserole or saucepan over a moderate heat and add the oil, then, after a few seconds, the butter. Tip in the carrots, stir, put a lid on the pan, turn the heat down a bit and leave for 5 minutes. Remove the lid, stir in the vegetable bouillon powder and 3 tablespoons of water and replace the lid. Cook over a low to medium heat for about 20 minutes until the carrots are tender, stirring them occasionally. Add more water if they appear to be sticking. Season with salt and pepper and stir in a spoonful of chopped parsley if you have some.

NOT-AT-ALL-BORING PEAS AND CARROTS

Peas and carrots are the vegetables most people think of when you talk about 'meat and two veg'. Here's a rather more sophisticated version than the original boil'em-to-death method – a variant on the previous recipe.

SERVES 4

450g carrots, preferably organic
1 tbsp light olive oil
15g butter
$\frac{1}{2}$ tsp ground coriander
$\frac{1}{2}$ tsp vegetable bouillon powder
200g frozen petits pois
2 tbsp finely chopped parsley

Peel the carrots and cut them in half horizontally, then cut the top half lengthways in two so all the pieces are roughly the same size. Slice them thinly. Heat a lidded casserole over a moderate heat and add the olive oil, then, after a few seconds, the butter.

Once the butter has melted tip in the sliced carrots and give them a stir. Sprinkle over the coriander and vegetable bouillon powder, stir, then pour in 75ml water. Bring to the boil then put a lid on the dish, turn the heat down and simmer for 15–20 minutes until the carrots are just cooked. Tip in the peas, bring back to a simmer then cook for another 5 minutes till the peas are tender. Stir in the parsley and serve.

SPICED CARROT AND SPRING ONION FRITTERS

An adaptation of a recipe from one of my favourite chefs, Shaun Hill, which jazzes up some cold meat and salad.

SERVES 2

50g coarsely grated carrot (preferably organic)
2–3 spring onions, trimmed and finely sliced (about 40g in total)
1 large egg, beaten
2 tablespoons fresh white breadcrumbs
$\frac{1}{4}$ tsp mild or medium-hot curry powder
Salt and freshly ground black pepper
Vegetable oil for frying

Put the carrot, spring onion, egg and breadcrumbs into a bowl and combine. Season with the curry powder, salt and pepper. Pour enough oil in a large frying pan to cover the base to a depth of about a centimetre. Heat until hot enough to quickly fry a cube of bread. Drop the mixture into the oil a tablespoon at a time – it should make about 7–8 fritters.
Turn them over after they've cooked about a minute and are nicely browned and give them a minute the other side. Drain for a few seconds on kitchen paper and eat immediately.

SWEDE AND CARROT MASH

Carrots alone don't make great mash but when combined with swede they certainly do.

SERVES 4

1 medium swede (about 500–550g), peeled and cut into small cubes
3 medium carrots (about 250–275g), peeled and sliced
1 litre hot vegetable stock made with 1 tbsp vegetable bouillon powder or a vegetable stock cube
25g butter
1 tbsp double or whipping cream (optional)
Salt, freshly ground black pepper and a little grated nutmeg

Put the cubed swede and carrot in a medium-sized saucepan and cover with the hot vegetable stock. Bring to the boil and simmer for about 20 minutes until the vegetables are soft. Strain, reserving the cooking water and put the vegetables in a food processor. Whizz them until smooth. Add the butter and 1–2 tablespoons of the vegetable cooking water and whizz again. Return to the pan and heat through gently, adding a little cream if you want it to taste richer and more luxurious. Season with salt, plenty of black pepper and a little freshly grated nutmeg. You can obviously also make swede mash on its own without the carrots.

GRILLED PARSNIPS WITH HONEY AND ROSEMARY

A healthy (well, quite healthy) alternative to chips.

SERVES 3–4

450g parsnips
2 tbsp of light olive oil or sunflower oil
2 tsp finely chopped fresh rosemary
2–3 tsp of honey
Salt and freshly ground black pepper

Peel the parsnips and cut into even-sized, chip-shaped pieces, removing the central woody core where necessary. Put in a saucepan, cover with boiling, salted water and cook for 5 minutes. Drain and lay the parsnips on a foil-lined grill pan or baking dish. Heat the grill. Spoon half the oil over the parsnips, sprinkle with half the rosemary and drizzle with half the honey. Grill until brown (about 3–4 minutes) then turn the parsnip pieces over, add the remaining oil, rosemary and honey and grill the other side. Sprinkle with salt and pepper and serve. Good with roast or grilled lamb or duck.

PARSNIP PUREE

Makes a fabulously luxurious mash.

SERVES 4–6

4 medium-sized parsnips (about 550–575g), preferably organic
1–2 tbsp double cream
Salt, pepper and freshly ground nutmeg

Peel the parsnips and cut into even-sized cubes, cutting away the central woody core where necessary. Put in a saucepan, cover with boiling water, add a little salt and bring back to the boil. Cook for about 15 minutes until the parsnips are soft then drain them thoroughly, reserving the cooking water. Cool for a few minutes then whizz the parsnips in a food processor or blender until absolutely smooth. Add 1 tablespoon of the cream and 3–4 tablespoons of the reserved cooking water until it looks seductively sloppy. Scoop it out of the food processor and back into the saucepan. Season with salt, pepper and freshly ground nutmeg. Add a little more cream or cooking water if you think it needs it and reheat gently. Good with rich dark beef and oxtail stews.

BAKED TURNIPS WITH CREAM AND PARMESAN

A turnipy version of gratin dauphinoise that works particularly well with roast or grilled lamb or duck. You can also cook turnips in a similar way to the Braised Carrots on p123, adding a little bit of sugar or honey for sweetness.

SERVES 4

750g turnips, peeled and finely sliced
1 litre hot vegetable stock made with
 1 tbsp vegetable bouillon
A little soft butter

1 clove of garlic
1 tsp fresh or $\frac{1}{2}$ tsp dried thyme
150ml of whipping cream
4 tbsp freshly grated Parmesan
15g chilled butter
Salt and freshly ground black pepper

Preheat the oven to 200C/400F/Gas 6. Put the turnips in a saucepan and cover with the hot stock. Bring to the boil and cook for 2 minutes. Reserve or discard the cooking water. Meanwhile, smear the butter generously over a gratin dish. Peel and half the garlic and rub over the inside of the dish. Tip the drained turnip slices into the dish, season with salt, pepper and thyme and toss together. Flatten out the surface, pour over the whipping cream and sprinkle over the Parmesan. Dot with the butter and bake for 15 minutes then turn the heat down to 190C/375F/Gas 5 and bake for another 15–20 minutes until the turnips are soft and the top nicely browned.

GRATIN OF BRUSSEL SPROUTS

Even sprout-haters will like this. Sprout lovers will be in ecstasies.

SERVES 4–6

1 litre hot vegetable stock made with
 1 tbsp vegetable bouillon powder
500g sprouts, trimmed
15g soft butter
100g (half a standard tub) crème
 fraîche
1 large egg, lightly beaten
25g freshly grated Parmesan
Salt and freshly ground black pepper
A little freshly grated nutmeg
 (optional)
10g fresh breadcrumbs

Pour the hot stock over the sprouts and bring back to the boil. Add salt, stir and simmer for about 8–10 minutes until just tender but still green. Drain them, reserving the stock. Tip the sprouts into a food processor and pulse 4 or 5 times until roughly chopped. Tip the sprouts into a shallow ovenproof dish, add the butter and stir. Mix the crème fraîche with 100ml of the stock, add the lightly beaten egg and half the Parmesan and season with salt, pepper and a little grated nutmeg. Pour over the chopped sprouts and mix well.

Mix the remaining Parmesan and breadcrumbs and sprinkle over the top of the gratin. Bake at 190C/375F/Gas 5 for 20 minutes.

STIR-FRIED SPROUTS WITH CASHEW NUTS

Another good way of jazzing up sprouts that works well with pork, chicken and other birds like guineafowl, pheasant and partridge and also with leftovers.

SERVES 2–3

250g sprouts
2 tbsp sunflower or light olive oil
25g broken or chopped cashew nuts
1 clove of garlic, peeled and crushed
1 tbsp light soy sauce

Trim the bottom and outer leaves off the sprouts and slice them thinly. Heat a wok, add the oil and heat through for around a minute until hot. Tip in the cashew nuts, fry for a few seconds and remove with a slotted spoon. Add the sprouts and stir-fry for about 3 minutes until just tender. Add the crushed garlic, soy and 2 tablespoons of water and cook for a few more seconds until the water has evaporated. Stir in the fried cashew nuts and serve.

HOT BUTTERED CABBAGE

The last thing you want to do with cabbage is to drown it or to cook it too long. This way it's delicious, especially with pork and gammon.

SERVES 3–4

1 small Hispi or Savoy cabbage
A good slice of butter
Salt and freshly ground black pepper

Remove any damaged outer leaves from the cabbage, cut it in quarters and cut away the hard central core. Slice thickly, put in a colander and rinse. Pour boiling water into the base of a large saucepan to a depth of about 2cm, bring back to the boil and tip in the cabbage. Cook fast for 2 minutes, turning it regularly until just tender. Drain, return to the pan and add the butter, season well with salt and pepper.

GARLIC GREENS

Dark greens combine really well with oil and garlic. Good with dark, rich stews.

SERVES 4–6

2 heads of spring greens
2 tbsp olive oil
1 large clove of garlic, peeled and crushed
Salt and freshly ground black pepper

Drop the greens into a bowl or sink full of cold water. Pull the leaves away from the stalk and tear out the central tough rib. Pack the leaves into a large saucepan, pour over a little boiling water, and bring back to the boil. Boil fast for 2 minutes, turning the leaves so they cook evenly, then tip the leaves into a colander. Heat the oil in the pan, add the garlic and place over a low heat for a couple of minutes so the garlic softens but doesn't colour. Tip the drained greens back in the pan and toss with the garlicky oil. Heat through for another couple of minutes, season with salt and pepper and serve.

STEAMED CABBAGE WEDGES WITH MELTED BUTTER

Another way of preparing cabbage that looks good with a large family roast. You can cook brussel tops (the tops of brussels sprouts) the same way.

SERVES 4 (OR 8 IF SERVING WITH OTHER VEGETABLES)

2 small Hispi or Savoy cabbages
40g butter
Salt and pepper

Remove the outer leaves of the cabbage, quarter and cut away the core as described in the previous recipe above. Put the cabbage quarters in a steamer (You should be able to fit in all the wedges if you have a steamer with a double basket, otherwise cook them in two batches). Cook until just tender (about 5–6 minutes). Transfer to a bowl. Melt the butter in a saucepan and pour over the cabbage wedges. Season with salt and pepper.

BUTTERED SPINACH WITH NUTMEG

One of my favourite vegetable dishes. Good with steak, grilled lamb and roast chicken. If you're using microwaveable bags of spinach follow the pack instructions, drain the spinach then follow the recipe below. Ditto with frozen leaf spinach. Cook it over a low heat without any extra water, drain it and add butter and seasoning as described.

SERVES 4

500g loose spinach leaves
15g butter
Salt, pepper and freshly grated
  nutmeg

Tip the leaves into a large bowl or sink full of cold water and give them a good swirl. Discard any damaged leaves and remove the central tough rib from the larger leaves. Drain the leaves and pack them into a large saucepan without any extra water. Put the pan over a low heat, cover and leave for about 5 minutes. Turn the leaves over (the bottom leaves should have collapsed), replace the lid and cook for another 3 to 4 minutes until all the leaves have collapsed but are still bright green. Drain the spinach thoroughly in a colander pressing out the excess water. Return the leaves to the pan and chop roughly. Add the butter and heat through. Season with salt, pepper and freshly grated nutmeg.

BRAISED RED CABBAGE

Long slow cooking makes red cabbage a natural partner for a dark, rich stew.

SERVES 8

1 medium red cabbage (about 1 kg)
3 tbsp olive oil
250g onions, peeled and sliced
1 large clove of garlic, peeled and
  crushed
1 large Bramley apple (about 300g)
1 tsp ground mixed spice

25g dark muscovado sugar
100 ml red wine
2 tbsp red wine vinegar
Salt and freshly ground black pepper

Cut the cabbage in quarters, peel off any outer leaves, cut away the white core at the base and shred finely. Heat the olive oil in a large lidded casserole or saucepan and fry the onions until beginning to soften. Add the garlic, stir then tip in the cabbage and mix thoroughly. Cook slowly for about 15 minutes until the cabbage starts to collapse. Quarter and peel the apple and slice it into the casserole. Add the mixed spice, sugar, wine, vinegar, salt and pepper, bring up to simmering point then put a lid on the pan. Turn the heat right down and cook the cabbage very gently for about 2^1/$_2$–3 hours stirring it occasionally. Season to taste with salt and pepper and a little more sugar if you find it too sharp. Any leftovers will freeze well.

FRIED CAULIFLOWER WITH ONION

We're so locked in to serving cauliflower with a cheese sauce it's easy to forget that there are other ways of cooking it, which, if truth be told, accentuate its flavour more. Frying it with onion is one.

SERVES 2

1 small cauliflower or ½ a larger one (about 450g of florets in total)
2 tbsp light olive or sunflower oil
1 small onion, peeled and finely chopped
1 clove of garlic, peeled and finely chopped
A small slice of butter (about 15g)
3 tbsp finely chopped fresh parsley
Salt and freshly ground black pepper

Cut the cauliflower up into small even-sized florets and steam or microwave them for 3 minutes. Drain if necessary. Heat a large saucepan or wok, heat the oil and fry the onion for about 3 minutes until starting to brown. Add the part-cooked cauliflower florets and stir-fry them for a couple of minutes then add the butter and continue to stir-fry over a low heat until the cauliflower is lightly browned. Stir in the parsley, season with salt and pepper and serve. Good with pork steaks or chops.

CAULIFLOWER CHEESE

One of the ubiquitous trio of vegetables – the others being red cabbage and ratatouille – that used to be served by restaurants in the '70's no matter what dish you ordered. Resist the temptation to make it too cheesy when you're serving it as an accompaniment.

SERVES 4

1 medium-sized cauliflower
25g butter
25g plain flour
350–400ml semi-skimmed milk
75g mature Cheddar, coarsely grated
Salt and white pepper

Cut the outside leaves off the cauliflower but keep any tender, inner leaves. Cut the florets off the stalk and divide them into even-sized clusters. Steam or boil the florets and inner leaves until just tender (about 6–7 minutes), drain and tip into a shallow buttered baking dish. Melt the butter gently in a small non-stick saucepan, stir in the flour and cook over a low heat for about 30 seconds. Take the pan off the heat and gradually add the milk bit by bit, stirring between each addition. When you've added half the milk you can pour most of the rest of the milk in one go, holding back a little to see if you need it.

Bring the sauce to the boil, turn the heat right down and simmer for 5 minutes until thick and smooth. Take off the heat and add half the cheese, season with salt and white pepper to taste. If the sauce is too thick add the remaining milk or a couple of spoonfuls of the water you've used for cooking the cauliflower. Preheat the grill to a high setting. Pour the sauce over the cauliflower florets, sprinkle with the remaining cheese and grill until the top is nicely crusted and brown (about 4 minutes). Particularly good with roast gammon or cold ham.

PURPLE SPROUTING BROCCOLI WITH BLOOD ORANGE BUTTER

Purple sprouting broccoli comes at just the right time of year (March/April) when one's tired of roots but spring vegetables haven't yet started.

SERVES 2–3

250g purple sprouting broccoli or a head of broccoli
25g butter
3 tbsp blood orange or ordinary orange juice
A little grated orange rind (about $\frac{1}{2}$ tsp)
$\frac{1}{2}$–1 tsp cider vinegar
Salt and pepper

Trim the broccoli and steam or microwave until just tender (3–4 minutes). Put the butter in a saucepan with the orange juice and rind and heat gently, stirring, until the butter has melted. Add cider vinegar to taste and season with salt and pepper. Transfer the broccoli to a small vegetable dish and pour over the orange butter. Very good with chicken or guinea fowl and lambs' liver.

WARM BROCCOLI 'SALAD'

Another way of adding zip to broccoli.

A head of broccoli
2 tbsp olive oil
1 clove of garlic, peeled and very finely chopped
$\frac{1}{2}$ tsp chilli flakes or a few twists of a hot spice grind
Salt, freshly ground black pepper and a squeeze of lemon juice

Trim the broccoli florets off the stalk and steam or microwave for 4 minutes until almost cooked. Add the oil to a frying pan over a moderate heat, add the garlic and chilli flakes and cook for a few seconds then tip in the broccoli florets and turn in the warm, flavoured oil. Season with salt and a little black pepper and tip into a serving dish. Cool for 10 minutes and serve. Good with grilled chicken or lamb chops.

FRENCH PEAS

The loss of colour you get from slow-cooking peas is more than compensated for by the intense sweetness and savouriness of this dish, which is almost a meal in itself. Perfect with duck.

SERVES 4–6

1 tbsp light olive or sunflower oil
15g butter
110g streaky bacon in a piece or 3–4 thickly sliced streaky bacon rashers, rind removed and chopped small (or diced pancetta)
$^2/_3$ of a bunch of spring onions, trimmed and sliced
$^1/_4$ tsp of paprika or sweet pimenton
450g frozen petits pois
150ml hot chicken or vegetable stock made with 1 tsp of vegetable bouillon powder
Outside leaves of a soft round lettuce, washed, dried and roughly chopped
Salt and pepper

Heat the oil and butter in a large lidded saucepan or casserole. Fry the bacon until the fat starts to run, then add the spring onions and cook for about 3–4 minutes until beginning to soften. Stir in the paprika then add the peas. Pour in the hot stock and bring up to simmering point. Partially cover the pan and leave to simmer for about 40–45 minutes, adding the lettuce about 10 minutes before the end of the cooking time. Season to taste with salt and pepper.

GARLICKY GREEN BEANS

The only way to cook those rather tasteless Kenya beans that sometimes seem just about the only fresh vegetable available.

SERVES 4–6

450g fine green beans, trimmed
2 tbsp olive oil
1 large clove of garlic, peeled and crushed
Salt and freshly ground black pepper

Pour a kettleful of boiling water into a saucepan and bring back to the boil. Tip in the beans, bring back to the boil again and cook for about 4–5 minutes or until tender but still green. Drain into a colander and rinse with cold water. Pour the oil into the saucepan, place over a low heat, add the garlic and stir. Cook for a couple of minutes until the garlic softens but don't let it colour. Tip the beans back in the pan and toss them in the garlicky oil. Heat through for another couple of minutes, season with salt and pepper and serve.

RUNNER BEAN PUREE

This purée really is the essence of summer. I could eat it every day. Particularly good with lamb cutlets or grilled chicken.

SERVES 3–4

500g runner beans
1/2 an onion, peeled and thinly sliced
500ml hot vegetable stock made with 1 1/2 tsp vegetable bouillon powder
15g butter
1 tbsp potato flakes
1 tsp chopped, fresh thyme or, even better, summer savory
2 tbsp whipping cream (optional)
Salt, pepper and lemon juice to taste

Top and tail the runner beans, cutting off the stringy edges if the beans are a bit elderly. Put them in a saucepan with the onion slices, pour over the hot stock, bring to the boil and cook for about 8–10 minutes until the beans are tender but still green. Drain the beans and onion, retaining the cooking liquid. Tip the vegetables into a food processor and whizz, adding a little of the cooking water to achieve a smooth consistency. Add the butter and potato flakes and whizz again. Transfer the mix to a saucepan and reheat gently. Add the thyme and cream, if using, or a little more cooking liquid if you're not. Season to taste with salt, pepper and a squeeze of lemon juice.

STEAMED SUMMER VEGETABLES WITH TOMATOES, PINENUTS AND BASIL

A summery warm vegetable salad that goes really well with cold rare roast beef. You could also add a few asparagus tips if available.

SERVES 4–6

200g fine green beans, trimmed
150g sugar snap peas or mangetout
150g baby courgettes, cut in half
   lengthways
3–4 tbsp extra virgin olive oil
40g pinenuts
250g cherry tomatoes
A handful of torn basil leaves
Salt, pepper and balsamic vinegar to
   serve

Steam the beans, sugar snap peas and courgettes separately until tender but still green (the beans will take about 8–9 minutes, the courgettes and the peas about 4–5). Tip them out into a large bowl or plate as they're ready. Heat the oil in a frying pan over a moderate heat, add the pinenuts and fry until they start to brown. Scoop out and add to the vegetables. Add the tomatoes to the pan, turn the heat up and shake over the heat for a couple of minutes until the skins start to split. Throw in the basil, stir and remove the pan from the heat. Tip the tomatoes, basil and oil over the other vegetables and toss together. Season with salt and pepper and drizzle over a teaspoon of balsamic vinegar and a little more oil if needed. Serve warm or cool.

RATATOUILLE

This Provencal vegetable stew became such a cliché in the 1970s when it was invariably accompanied by such totally incompatible vegetables as cauliflower cheese and red cabbage that it vanished off the culinary map. But make it in season (late summer) and serve it simply and you'll see what the fuss was all about.

SERVES 6–8

150–175ml extra virgin olive oil

3 medium-sized sweet onions, peeled and finely sliced

1 medium red pepper quartered, seeded and sliced

1 medium green pepper, quartered, seeded and sliced

2 medium courgettes, trimmed and thickly sliced

1 medium-sized aubergine, cut into small cubes

2 large cloves of garlic, peeled and finely chopped

1 tbsp chopped fresh marjoram or oregano or 1 tsp dried marjoram or oregano

$\frac{1}{2}$ tsp paprika (optional)

1 rounded tbsp tomato purée

400g ripe round or plum tomatoes, skinned and roughly chopped (or a 400g tin of chopped tomatoes but leave out the tomato purée)

8–10 large basil leaves

Sea salt, freshly ground black pepper and wine vinegar to taste

Heat 3 tbsp of the oil in a lidded casserole or saucepan, add the sliced onion, stir, cover and cook over a low heat, stirring occasionally for about 10–15 minutes while you fry the rest of the vegetables. Heat 2 tablespoons of oil over a moderately high heat in a wok or large frying pan and stir-fry the peppers for a couple of minutes until beginning to brown. Remove with a slotted spoon and set aside. Add another tablespoon of oil and fry the sliced courgettes for another couple of minutes, turning them every few seconds. Remove from the pan with a slotted spoon, add 2 more tablespoons of oil and fry the aubergine, stirring it constantly until it starts to brown. Set aside with the peppers and courgettes.

Add the garlic, marjoram and paprika to the onions, stir and cook for a minute then stir in the tomato purée. Cook for another minute then add the tomatoes. Bring to the boil and simmer for 3–4 minutes until they start to break down and add 3 tablespoons of water. Add the peppers, courgettes and aubergines to the pan, stir then turn the heat right down, cover and cook for about 1–1$\frac{1}{4}$ hours until the vegetables are soft but still retain their shape. Cool for 15 minutes then stir in an extra couple of spoonfuls of olive oil. Season generously with salt and pepper and a few drops of wine vinegar. Roughly tear the basil leaves and stir them in. Serve warm with grilled or roast lamb or cold with leftovers.

COURGETTE AND TOMATO GRATIN

A nice, light summery accompaniment for some grilled lamb steaks or chops.

SERVES 4

3–4 tbsp extra virgin olive oil
400g courgettes, trimmed and diagonally sliced
1 medium onion, peeled and thinly sliced
1 small clove of garlic, peeled and crushed
300g ripe tomatoes, sliced (preferably Pomodorino)
5–6 large basil leaves or 1 tsp fresh thyme
2 tbsp Parmesan cheese
1 tbsp natural breadcrumbs

Preheat the oven to 190C/375F/ Gas 5. Heat a large frying pan, add 2 tablespoons of the oil then fry the courgette slices in a single layer for 2–3 minutes a side until lightly browned. (You will probably have to do this in two batches, adding a little more oil as needed). Remove the courgettes from the pan with a slotted spoon then fry the onion in the remaining oil until soft and beginning to colour (about 4–5 minutes). Add the crushed garlic and stir. Lightly oil a shallow baking dish and layer the vegetables, starting with the courgettes, then the onions, then tomatoes. Add half the basil leaves, roughly torn, sprinkle over a tablespoon of the Parmesan and season with salt and pepper then layer the remaining vegetables and seasoning finishing with a layer of courgettes. Add a tablespoon of water to stop the vegetables catching. Mix the remaining Parmesan with the dried breadcrumbs and sprinkle over the surface of the courgettes then drizzle over a little extra oil. Bake uncovered for 30–35 minutes until the vegetables are cooked and the top nice and crusty.

COURGETTE 'CHIPS'

A good alternative to potatoes in summer.

SERVES 2–3

250g courgettes
1 tbsp plain flour
3 tbsp olive oil
Salt and pepper

Trim the courgettes at each end, halve lengthways and cut into chip-sized pieces. Put the flour in a shallow bowl, season with salt and pepper and toss the courgette 'chips' in the flour. Heat a medium-sized frying pan, add the oil and heat for a couple of minutes then fry the 'chips' swiftly on all sides until lightly browned, moving them around with a spatula. Scoop them out of the pan, tilting the pan away from you to avoid picking up too much oil, sprinkle with salt and serve.

ONE-MINUTE COURGETTES

The only way my eldest daughter will eat courgettes. Without the mint, obviously.

SERVES 2

2–3 medium courgettes
1 tbsp olive oil
25g butter, cut into cubes
1 tbsp chopped fresh mint leaves
  (optional)
Salt and pepper

Trim and coarsely grate the courgettes. Heat a medium-sized frying pan over a high heat, add the oil, then when it's hot, the cubed butter. Tip in the courgettes and fry for a minute until just cooked. Stir in the mint, if using, and season with salt and pepper.

ROAST BUTTERNUT SQUASH

With its vivid orange colour, butternut squash always looks great. Serve on a large platter for maximum effect.

SERVES 4–8

1 tsp coriander seeds
1/2 tsp chilli flakes
1/2 tsp coarse sea salt
1/4 tsp black peppercorns
2 medium-sized butternut squash
2 tbsp olive oil

Preheat the oven to 190C/375F/Gas 5. Grind together the coriander seeds, chilli flakes, salt and pepper with a pestle and mortar. Rinse and dry the outside of the squash, quarter them and scoop out the seeds. Put the squash, skin-side downwards into a roasting tin, trickle over the olive oil and season with the spice mix. Roast for about 35–40 minutes until tender but not too soft. Good with dark, sticky braises or roasts.

A GOOD OLD-FASHIONED ENGLISH SALAD

This is what invariably used to be served up as a salad in the 'fifties, usually made well ahead so the beetroot (which was pickled, not freshly cooked) oozed all over the salad cream (Heinz, of course) and turned it an unappetising pink. Now you can buy top quality ingredients for it in your farmer's market. It deserves another outing as the ideal partner for cold ham and new potatoes.

SERVES 4

2 Little Gem lettuces
250g cherry tomatoes, halved
1/3 of a cucumber, peeled and thinly
  sliced
1/2 a bunch of spring onions, trimmed
3–4 beetroot, roasted (see below) or
cooked vacuum-packed
A small handful of chives

FOR THE DRESSING
2 level tsp English mustard
1 level tsp unrefined caster sugar
2 tbsp malt vinegar
4 tbsp sunflower or grapeseed oil
2 level tbsp crème fraîche
A small pinch of ground turmeric
Sea salt, white pepper, and a couple
  of drops of Worcestershire sauce

First make the dressing. Put the mustard and caster sugar in a bowl with a little salt and white pepper, add 1 tbsp of vinegar and whisk together. Gradually whisk in the remaining vinegar, oil and crème fraîche. Leave for 5–10 minutes while you prepare and assemble the salad then check the seasoning adding more salt, sugar if it needs it and a tiny pinch of turmeric to deepen the colour.

Wash and dry the lettuce. Peel and thinly slice the cucumber. Trim the onions and slice lengthwise into two or four depending how big they are. Quarter the beetroot. Halve the tomatoes. Arrange the salads on individual plates, or on a big shallow platter, starting with the lettuce, then the cucumber, spring onions, beetroot and tomatoes. Spoon over the dressing and sprinkle with chopped chives. Serve with generous chunks of cold ham, carved off the bone and warm, buttered new potatoes tossed with finely chopped parsley.

ROAST BEETROOT

Heat the oven to 200C/400F/Gas 6. Cut off the beet tops and trim off the roots. Wash the beets under running water to remove any dirt and dry with a kitchen paper. Take a large piece of foil and place it on a baking tray. Oil it lightly, place the beets in the middle and scrunch the edges of the foil together to make a loose tent. Place on a baking tray and cook the beets for about an hour, or until tender. When cool enough to handle, peel off the skin and cut the beets into quarters or smaller wedges.

A SIMPLE LETTUCE SALAD

Using bags of mixed salad leaves makes you forget how good fresh lettuce really is.

SERVES 4

A Cos or Webbs lettuce or 2 round
   lettuces or 3 Little Gem lettuces

FOR THE VINAIGRETTE DRESSING

1 tsp Dijon mustard
1 tbsp wine vinegar
4 tbsp extra virgin olive oil
Salt, freshly ground black pepper and
   a small pinch of sugar
A small handful of chives (optional)

Remove any damaged and dirty outer leaves from the lettuce. Pull off the other leaves and wash them in a large bowl or sink full of cold water. Place in a salad spinner or lay them on a clean tea-towel and pat them dry. Put the mustard in a salad bowl with the vinegar and season with salt and pepper and whisk together with a fork. Gradually add the oil whisking all the time so that it thickens. Whisk in a tablespoon of water. Check the seasoning adding more salt, pepper and sugar to taste if you feel it needs any or all of these. Just before you want to eat the salad, add the leaves to the bowl then toss the leaves over in the dressing so that each leaf is lightly coated. Snip over some chives if using.

CUCUMBER AND CHIVE SALAD

A very delicate, typically English salad – perfect for cold chicken.

SERVES 6

1 cucumber, peeled and finely sliced
2 tbsp tarragon vinegar
2 level tbsp scissor snipped chives
$1/4$ tsp caster sugar plus extra to taste
Fine sea salt and freshly ground black
   pepper

Place the cucumber on a large flat dinner plate or soup plate and sprinkle with a teaspoon of sea salt. Place another plate on top of the cucumber and weight it with a heavy tin or other weight. After about 30 minutes, drain off any liquid that has formed, rinse the cucumber and pat dry with kitchen paper.

Place in a shallow dish, sprinkle over the sugar, tarragon vinegar and chopped chives and mix well. Season with freshly ground black pepper and extra sugar if you think it needs it.

WATERCRESS, ORANGE AND WALNUT SALAD

Watercress hardly gets a look-in these days, we're all so smitten with rocket, but if you buy it fresh from a farmer's market or, even better, direct from a watercress grower you'll wonder why you don't eat it more often.

SERVES 3–4

2 oranges
4 tbsp olive oil
A bunch of fresh watercress
50g broken walnuts
Salt and freshly ground black pepper

Peel one of the oranges by scoring it in quarters round the outside and plunging it in boiling water for 3–4 minutes. Drain off the water and peel away the rind and as much pith as possible. Cut into thick slices and then into small triangular segments, again removing any excess pith. Squeeze the juice from the other orange and whisk with the olive oil. Season with salt and pepper. When ready to serve, divide the watercress between the plates, scatter over the orange pieces and walnuts and spoon over the dressing. Good with cold pork, chicken or duck.

RUSSIAN SALAD

A real blast from the past, Russian salad – a salad of mixed vegetables with mayonnaise – is hardly ever seen these days but it makes a change from the usual potato salad.

SERVES 4–6

1–2 small turnips
1–2 medium-sized carrots
100g whole green beans (not the fine ones)
250g new potatoes, scrubbed but with the skins left on
1/2 tin of flageolet beans, drained and rinsed
1/2 a small onion, finely chopped
1–2 pickled cucumbers, finely chopped
2 tbsp Vinaigrette Dressing (see p150)
2 tbsp mayonnaise
A few finely snipped chives and/or 2 tbsp finely chopped parsley
Salt and pepper

Scrub the potatoes, leaving the skins on, and cut into quarters or halves. Peel the turnip and carrot and cut into similar sized pieces. Top and tail the beans and cut into short lengths. Cook the vegetables in boiling water until just tender (about 8–10 minutes), drain and refresh with cold water. Dice the vegetables and mix with the flageolet beans, onion and pickled cucumber. Pour the vinaigrette over and leave for 15 minutes to absorb. Mix the mayonnaise with a little of the liquid from the pickled cucumbers, pour over the salad, add the chives and/or parsley and toss together. Add extra seasoning if you think it needs it and serve. Good with cold pork, chicken or ham.

MEAT & VEG MATCHING

Stuck for an idea of which veg to serve? Here's a quick list of suggestions, including herbs and fruits that work well. Feel free to chop and change about though – this isn't a set of rules. (Potatoes obviously go with everything so I haven't mentioned them). See also the suggestions to go with cold meat on p110.

BEEF

Mushrooms, carrots, onions, parsnips, swedes, red cabbage, green beans, peas, tomatoes

Rocket, thyme

LAMB

Aubergine, courgettes, red peppers, onions, peas, green beans, runner beans, spinach, parsnips, carrots

Mint, rosemary, redcurrants, apricots

PORK

Cabbage and other greens, sprouts, cauliflower, mushrooms, leeks, celery, fennel, beans, sweet potatoes, squash, red peppers

Sage, apples, pears, apricots

GAMMON/HAM

Leeks, broad beans, peas, corn, carrots, cauliflower

Parsley

CHICKEN

Peas, carrots, courgettes, broccoli, beans, broad beans, asparagus, leeks, fennel, celery, chicory, mushrooms, spinach, peppers, tomatoes, corn, Cos lettuce, cucumber

Parsley, tarragon, thyme, apples, lemon

DUCK

Peas, turnips, parsnips, cabbage and other greens, broccoli, watercress

Oranges, cherries, plums, blackberries

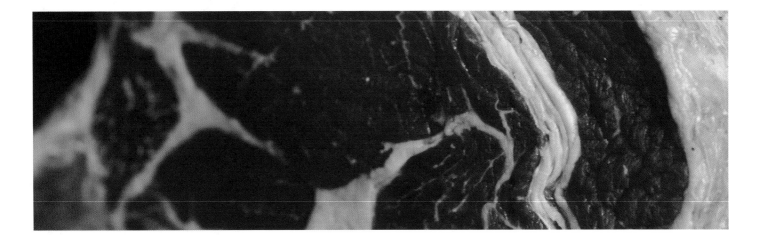

SUPPLIERS

Obviously you'll have your own local butcher – who I do urge you to use or you'll lose him – but if you're looking for one, check out the website of the quality-conscious Q Guild www.guildofqbutchers.com. I'm also a big fan of the Ginger Pig which trades in Borough Market and Moxon Street, off Marylebone High Street in London (020 7935 7788).

GOOD ONLINE AND MAIL ORDER SUPPLIERS

BROWN COW ORGANICS
WWW.BROWNCOWORGANICS.CO.UK
Much-awarded Somerset-based organic producer – a favourite of Hugh Fearnley-Whittingstall's.

DONALD RUSSELL
WWW.DONALDRUSSELL.COM
Well-established internet business, built on Scottish beef but now offering many other products. Particularly high standard of butchery.

HERITAGE PRIME
WWW.HERITAGEPRIME.CO.UK
Not just organic but biodynamic. Great pork.

HIGHER HACKNELL FARM
WWW.HIGHERHACKNELL.CO.UK
Another top West country organic meat producer.

NORTHFIELD FARM
WWW.NORTHFIELDFARM.COM
Rutland-based farm specialising in flavoursome rare breeds. Has stall at Borough Market in London.

PEDIGREE MEATS
WWW.HUNTSHAM.COM
Popular with chefs and others for rare-breed meats including fantastic Middle White pig.

SHEEPDROVE FARM, LAMBOURN, BERKS.
WWW.SHEEPDROVESHOP.COM
One of the biggest organic meat suppliers with a good range of products and fair prices, especially for cheaper cuts.

THE WELL HUNG MEAT COMPANY
WWW.WELLHUNGMEAT.COM
Winner of Organic Industry Award 2006 for best delivery/internet service.

VEG BOXES

RIVERFORD ORGANICS
WWWW.RIVERFORD.CO.UK
Reliable Devon-based supplier with an excellent website.

SUNNYFIELDS ORGANICS
WWW.SUNNYFIELDS.CO.UK
Very good Southampton-based producer delivering to Hampshire, parts of Surrey, Dorset and Greater London.

OTHER SUPPLIERS

DORSET PASTRY
WWW.DORSETPASTRY.COM
Probably better than any pastry you could make yourself.

WENDY BRANDON
WWW.WENDYBRANDON.CO.UK
Gorgeous home-made tasting chutneys for cold meats.

NATIONAL ASSOCIATION OF FARMER'S MARKETS
WWW.FARMERSMARKETS.NET
Find your nearest one.

INDEX

ACKNOWLEDGEMENTS

Thanks to my two local butchers, butchers of the old school, for their advice and support – Joe Collier of Eastwood Butchers in Berkhamsted and Barry of W. Hall in Redbourn. To my family (come on, you enjoyed this one...), to my patient and long-suffering publisher Absolute Press (thanks, yet again, Jon, Meg and Matt) and to photographer Jason Lowe and food stylist Claire Ptak who made these recipes look just the way I wanted them to. No, better.

CONVERSION TABLE

Do keep to either metric or imperial measures throughout the whole recipe. Mixing the two can lead to all kinds of problems.

25g	1 oz	275g	10 oz	5ml	1 tsp
50g	2 oz	300g	11 oz	15ml	1 tbsp
75g	3 oz	350g	12 oz	150ml	$1/4$ pint
100g	4 oz	375g	13 oz	300ml	$1/2$ pint
150g	5 oz	400g	14 oz	450ml	$3/4$ pint
175g	6 oz	425g	15 oz	600ml	1 pint
200g	7 oz	450g	16 oz (1lb)	1.2l	2 pints
225g	8 oz	1kg	2 lb		
250g	9 oz